*Knowing Our Faith*

# Knowing Our Faith

*A Guide for Believers, Seekers,*
*and Christian Communities*

Justo L. González

WILLIAM B. EERDMANS PUBLISHING COMPANY
GRAND RAPIDS, MICHIGAN

Wm. B. Eerdmans Publishing Co.
4035 Park East Court SE, Grand Rapids, Michigan 49546
www.eerdmans.com

Previously published as *Conoce tu fe: Cristianismo para el siglo XXI,*
ISBN 978-1-945339-09-7 (print edition) and ISBN 978-1-945339-10-3 (electronic
edition), © 2017 Asociación para la Educación Teológica Hispana (AETH).

25  24  23  22  21  20  19        1  2  3  4  5  6  7

ISBN 978-0-8028-7706-2

**Library of Congress Cataloging-in-Publication Data**

A catalog record for this book is available from the Library of Congress.

I do not intend, Lord, to reach thy sublime height, for my mind is nothing when compared to it. But *I do wish in some way to understand your truth, the truth that my heart believes and loves*. I do not seek to understand in order to believe, but rather believe in order to understand.

Anselm of Canterbury, *Proslogion*

# Contents

# Preface

This book was born out of a growing concern on the part of church leaders in Puerto Rico, and some others elsewhere, that there is a need for introductory material to the Christian faith that, while recognizing the existence of various denominations and theological positions, is in fact an introduction to Christianity as it is generally held and understood by the church catholic. This idea began at a meeting sponsored by the Inter-American University of Puerto Rico and by the Association for Hispanic Theological Education (AETH) that brought together leaders from various denominations and church institutions in Puerto Rico. I was invited to write the book, and to send each chapter to representatives chosen by those denominations so that they could comment on what I had written and thus help me produce the book they had intended. I took their suggestions and corrections into account as I prepared the final draft of the manuscript.

The result of these efforts is a book published originally in Spanish under the auspices of the Inter-American University of Puerto Rico and AETH, but also with the endorsement of a wide variety of denominations. These include the Christian Church (Disciples of Christ) of Puerto Rico, the Methodist Church of Puerto Rico, the Church of the Nazarene, the Evangelical Lutheran Church, the Pentecostal Church of Jesus Christ, M. I., the Baptist churches of Puerto Rico, the Church of God (Cleveland), and the Presbytery of San Juan of the Presbyterian Church in the USA, as well as a number of agencies and institutions in Puerto Rico: the Bible Society, the Theological University of the Caribbean, and the regional office of the Latin American Council of Churches. After its original publication, several other bodies have also endorsed it for their use.

In translating the book, I have followed my usual practice of seeking to adapt the material to a different audience, but at the same time trying to remain as close to the original as possible. I may have succeeded or not. But in any case, I now offer this book to an English reading public not so much as my own work, but rather as a gift from the church in Puerto Rico to the rest of the church in other parts of the world. We—the churches and institutions that originally sponsored it, and myself—trust that, by the grace of God, this material will prove useful.

# An Open Letter to the Reader

Esteemed Reader:

Knowledge, pure reason, or logic seldom lead directly to faith. This is so because, in the final analysis, faith isn't a human work, but the work of the Holy Spirit in us. If you have faith, this isn't primarily because you've been convinced through rational arguments, but rather because the Holy Spirit has worked in you. Clearly, there are cases in which reason opens the way, tearing down obstacles that would otherwise keep you from faith. Thus, for instance, throughout history Christians have developed very strong arguments against polytheism, and those arguments have helped many by opening for them the way to faith. But if a polytheist is converted, the main reason for this is the work of the Holy Spirit in that person's heart. This is why there are so many and so frequent testimonies of Christians who, when they least expected it nor even sought it, came to the knowledge of Jesus Christ.

But this doesn't mean that the mind and its understanding have no place in the life of faith. On the contrary, our

xi

Lord Jesus Christ tells us that the first and greatest commandment includes loving God with the entire mind. It's not a matter of the mind leading us to faith; rather, faith leads us to make use of our mind according to the will of God. Quite possibly no one has expressed this more clearly or profoundly than our brother in the faith Anselm of Canterbury. Almost ten centuries ago, in a prayer at the opening of one of his books, he said, "I do not intend, Lord, to reach thy sublime height, for my mind is nothing when compared to it. But I do wish in some way to understand your truth, the truth that my heart believes and loves. I do not seek to understand in order to believe, but rather believe in order to understand." What Anselm says in these words is, first, that it isn't necessary to understand in order to believe; and, secondly, that whoever truly believes tries to understand. Let us look at these two points in order.

First, it is clear that it isn't necessary to understand in order to believe. If your experience is similar to that of millions of believers, most likely you came to faith not because someone convinced you with irrefutable arguments, but rather because the Holy Spirit moved you to faith. Understanding came later, as you inquired into the things of the Lord. When someone falls in love, it isn't because irrefutable arguments convince one that this is the person whom one should love, or because, after careful calculations, one comes to the conclusion that this is the best person with whom to share life. One falls in love simply because one does, by a sort of unexplainable "because." Similarly, one attains faith not through a series of rational arguments proving it, but rather because the Holy Spirit, in an also unexplainable "because," leads one to faith. It is folly to try to have faith without the help of God.

The second point follows from the first: Whoever really believes seeks to understand. Even apart from the commandment telling us to do so, we wish to understand faith because it has become the center of our lives, and we cannot help thinking and pondering on it. Likewise, when one falls in love, even though this happens for reasons that the mind cannot understand, one seeks to understand the beloved more deeply. To say "I love you very much, but I don't care who or how you are, or what you like, or even to understand you better" would be considered insensitive hypocrisy. Furthermore, if one doesn't know the beloved, one will have wrong expectations from that person. Likewise, whoever has faith cannot simply say to God, "I love you, Lord, but I don't really care to know much about who you are and how you are, because it's enough to love you and to believe in you." This is why Anselm says that "I do wish in some way to understand your truth, the truth that my heart believes and loves."

All of this should clarify the purpose of this book. I do not hope to convince you so that you will believe. That is to be left to the Holy Spirit. I write to you because you share the faith by which I live. I write so that you may share my joy in seeking to understand better this truth that our hearts believe and love.

But even though, up to this point, I have spoken to you in the singular, Christian faith is always lived in community. Our brother John Wesley, who lived in England some three hundred years ago, repeatedly declared that it is impossible to be a solitary Christian. Sometimes some of our brothers and sisters in the faith have thought that the best way to live the Christian life was to withdraw from the rest of the world in order to seek holiness by oneself. In the end, they were reminded that, according to Jesus, the second-highest commandment—after the love of God—is the love of neighbor. To fulfill this commandment, we have to live in community, in relationships among ourselves, mutually supporting and correcting one another. As we shall see further on, this means that the church, the community of faith, is a fundamental and unavoidable element in Christian life. For the present, let it suffice to say that if you wish to benefit further from this book, it may be good to read it together with other brothers and sisters. Take them at least as seriously as you take this book—or, even better, more seriously. It is these people, in the very process of your studying together, who will most help you understand this faith that your heart believes and loves. Most probably you will learn much more from these companions in the journey than you will from this or any other book. This is why, at the end of each chapter, there is a series of questions for discussion. It is my hope that such discussion and sharing will help us not only to understand our faith better, but also and above all to live it better.

Therefore, I invite you to read this book, perhaps in the quiet of your own home; but I also invite you to discuss it with other sisters and brothers in the faith, and to do so in the same spirit in which that already quoted ancestor in our faith, Anselm, said that he did not seek to understand in order to believe, but rather to believe in order to understand more fully this faith that our hearts believe and love.

May the Lord bless you and those who walk with you along the same journey.

# Understanding the Faith

## The Changing Church

Churches today are facing crises that were not expected six or seven decades ago. For sixteen centuries the church did not have to be greatly concerned about the knowledge of the faith that most people had. Society was generally Christian, and even though in many places there was a separation between church and state, the institutions of society—schools, social mores, family traditions, politics—helped the public at large know much of what Christianity is about. In most Western societies, believers as well nonbelievers knew the essentials of biblical teaching, the commandments, and the stories of Jesus and his disciples.

The result of this was that the church didn't have to do much—or thought it didn't have to do much—by way of basic Christian education. Those who came to the church knew much of its teachings and what these were about. In those conditions, it seemed enough to have Sunday school and perhaps a Bible study once a week for those who sought a bit more understanding. If a new person wished to join the church, a few classes would suffice, and many of these didn't have to do as much with general Christian doctrine as with a particular denomination's doctrinal emphases and form of government.

Today things have changed drastically. Increasingly we find people in our society who have little or no idea of what Christianity is. Christmas is about gifts and spending money, and Easter is about bunnies and chocolate eggs. In that setting, Christianity is about preserving morality and gaining access to heaven.

Yet, despite those changes, most of our more traditional churches still continue the old patterns and practices in the preparation of candidates for church membership. Even today, if you wish to join a Methodist church, you hear more about connectionalism, annual conferences, bishops, committees, and John Wesley than you hear about the central tenets of Christianity. If you wish to join a Presbyterian church, you hear more about the Presbyterian form of government and the distinctive doctrinal emphases of the Reformed tradition than you hear about the central tenets of Christianity. Apparently we imagine that people already know what Christianity is all about, that they understand the challenges of being a Christian in today's world, and that they just need to learn what it means to be a Methodist or a Presbyterian.

Meanwhile, a number of factors—particularly demographic changes—have radically changed the shape of the church. Here in the United States I note this particularly in

Latino Protestant churches. In places where, three or four decades ago, there were only one or two congregations, usually with twenty or thirty people, now there are dozens of churches, many of them with hundreds of members. Most of these are Pentecostal or independent churches. But, even though a quick glance would seem to indicate that these churches don't face the challenges of the more traditional denominations, the fact is that they too find themselves in dire need of more knowledge of the faith. The challenges that they face within the society in which they exist are many. Conditions in their communities are often disastrous, and not improving. It's not just a matter of crime and joblessness, but also of existing at the edge of the law, often in fear of deportation, of growing violence both in families and in the community at large, and of an unemployment rate that results in poverty and sometimes also in hunger and theft.

Furthermore, in the midst of these conditions, churches are constantly bombarded by strange doctrines and supposed "discoveries" regarding the Bible and its message. In the media we also find various distortions of Christianity. For many people in the United States, when someone declares that he or she is a Christian, this has to do much more with a political stance than with a faith or a religious experience or commitment. And this view is not altogether wrong, for—in many of the churches that are growing most rapidly—little is said about the significance of the cross, resurrection, and ascension of Jesus Christ, and much is said about the corruption of society and the need to avoid it or correct it. In some of the Latino churches I know best, one constantly hears that if one suffers, it is for lack of faith—a response that apparently ignores the sufferings of Jesus himself, the witness of the martyrs, and the many difficulties facing our ancestors in the faith. Some take this view to the point of promising believers that if they tithe and have faith, they will enjoy economic prosperity. Others claim to have discovered the mysterious key that tells them exactly the date and time when the Lord will return. And still others claim that their faith is such that they can demand that God do what they wish, and God will do it. Obviously, in churches where there is little knowledge of the faith, believers find themselves at a loss as to how to respond to such claims.

In all this we find ourselves in a situation similar to that of the church during its first centuries. At that point the church couldn't count on society at large to educate its people in the Christian faith. Just as in today's schools and in today's media one hears about Rudolph the red-nosed reindeer and about eggs and bunnies, but not about Jesus Christ, so in ancient times one would hear about Zeus, Poseidon, or Athena, but not about Jesus Christ. The early church had to find ways to teach and form its members. And so does the church today.

Even though some of us in the more traditional denominations don't realize it, Christianity is growing by leaps and bounds in minority communities. And in this too the situation of the church today is similar to that of the early centuries, when Christianity grew rapidly in spite of persecution and marginalization. That growth was so rapid that today it's impossible to establish how Christianity reached several of the large cities of the Roman Empire, let alone how it reached more remote places. For a number of reasons, Christianity was attractive to many during those early centuries—just as it is attractive today to many, particularly among ethnic minorities. But that very attractiveness, and its consequent growth, led to the proliferation of strange doctrines and practices that threatened the very heart of Christianity. Some said that Jesus Christ didn't really come in the flesh, but was a sort of spiritual phantom, a purely celestial being with the semblance of a body, and that therefore his sufferings weren't real. Others claimed that the contrast between the Old Testament and the New is such that each proclaims a different God, and therefore the god of creation, of Abraham, Sarah, and the prophets, is not the supreme God of Christians. And still others claimed to have secret knowledge that provided the only key to salvation.

The church responded to such confusion by making sure that its members knew and understood their faith in such a way that they could not be led away by every wind of doctrine. This was done mostly through an entire system of preparation for baptism, so that any who would join the church would be able to discern between true and false doctrine. Usually this preparation lasted at least two years; but at the end of the process the church could rest assured that those joining it knew what they were doing, and what the cost could be.

The purpose of this book is somewhat similar to that. We will not be dealing with complex matters or abstract speculation. Instead, we will be dealing with what is and has been the faith of the Christian church through the centuries, and why those doctrines are important for us today. Our purpose is to follow the advice in 1 Peter 3:15: "Always be ready to make your defense to anyone who demands from you an accounting for the hope that is in you." And our purpose is also to understand why we should not be led astray by any of the teeming false gods of our day.

## What Is Faith?

The word "faith" has at least two similar but different meanings. On the one hand, when we speak about having faith, we're not referring primarily to what we think or believe, but rather to a trust in the one in whom we believe. If a student says that he has faith in his professor, what he means is not that he's sure that his professor exists, but rather that he trusts what she tells him and explains to him. Likewise, when we say that we have faith in God, this doesn't mean primarily that we believe that God exists, but rather that we trust in God. Naturally, in order to trust the professor, the student has to be convinced that she exists; and similarly, in order to have faith in God, we have to be convinced that God exists. But knowing that the professor exists is not the same as having faith in her; and believing that God exists is not the same as having faith in God.

Along these lines, it's interesting to note that the confession of faith that we call the Apostles' Creed does not say "I believe that" but rather "I believe in." It is possible to believe that there is a God who is the creator of all things, that his Son took flesh in Jesus Christ, who lived, died, and rose again, and that the Holy Spirit is God, and yet not to have faith in this God in whose existence one believes. Having faith requires believing *in*: *in* God the Father Almighty; *in* Jesus Christ, his Son; and *in* the Holy Spirit.

This may require some explanation. Believing "in" means first of all to rest on the one in whom we believe. It is a matter of trusting that one. Believing "that" means affirming—sometimes simply admitting the possibility—that something may be true. If I say "I believe that it will rain tomorrow," I'm only expressing an opinion, or perhaps a hope or a fear. But I have no intention of committing my entire life to that rain that I believe will be coming. Likewise, one who says "I believe that God exists" simply is affirming a thought, but is not declaring a willingness to place all of life in the hands of this God. The Epistle of James says it quite clearly: "You believe that God is one; you do well. Even the demons believe—and shudder" (2:19). The demons believe that God exists, but they do not believe in God.

On the other hand, when we say that we believe "in" God, if we understand properly what we're saying, we're declaring ourselves ready to trust our lives to this God. It's not merely a matter of knowing that there is a God, but also and above all of being convicted that this God is such as to deserve our full trust. (Perhaps, to make this clear, we should sometimes say that we believe *on* God!)

In everyday life, we often use the words "in" and "on" in this sense of a trust and a reality that define us. If we say that we're on land, we mean that our feet are being sustained by that land. If we say that we're in the theater or in New York, we're saying that the theater or the city of New York is the reality in which we find our present being.

7

It is for this reason that the New Testament frequently speaks of being *in* Christ. This doesn't mean simply believing that Christ exists, or even that he died and was raised again. It certainly implies that and much more; but the emphasis lies on being in Christ in the same manner in which we are in a theater whose reality defines us, or on a land that physically sustains us.

Furthermore, being *in* also implies being surrounded by or submerged in something. Thus we say that fish live in the sea and that we live in the atmosphere. It is also in this sense that we must understand the biblical references to being *in* Christ. Being in Christ means being submerged in him, having him surround us just as water surrounds the fish.

In summary, faith is first of all a "believing *in*." It is trust in this God in whom we believe. It is abandoning ourselves to the arms of that God, knowing that this God's love and power are such that our lives are secure.

This is made clear in a famous interview that John Wesley had with another pastor in Georgia, long after he had studied theology and had been ordained, but still found no peace in his faith. Wesley reports that this other pastor . . .

> . . . asked, "Do you know Jesus Christ?" I paused, and said, "I know he is the Saviour of the world." "True," replied he; "but do you know he has saved you?" I answered, "I hope he has died to save me." He only added, "Do you know yourself?" I said, "I do." But I fear they were vain words. (*Journal*, March 7, 1736)

8

In other words, Wesley believed "that," but not quite "in." And this wasn't enough.

Still, it is true that in order to "believe in," it is necessary to "believe that." Obviously one cannot place full trust in a God whose very existence is not certain. The student mentioned earlier cannot trust his professor if he is not at least convinced that she exists, that she knows what she's talking about, and that she speaks the truth. Likewise, in order to believe in God in the strict sense of that phrase, we also need to be convinced not only that God exists, but also that this is a powerful and loving God. Thus, while it is true that "believing in" is much more than "believing that," it is also true that the first cannot exist without the second, and that each of the two contributes to the other.

What one believes in, and how one does so, has much to do with life and experience. A child trusts its mother—believes in her. But that trust is based on the multitude of occasions and experiences through which the child has learned about its mother. These experiences lead the child to trust her as good, caring, and other such characteristics. In other words, in order to trust in its mother, the child has to know and to believe that the mother is loving and will protect and defend it. If, on the other hand, a child sees twisted values in its mother, its trust in her will simply lead the child astray. In order really to believe in its mother, the child has to know her. And much of what the child does in trusting its mother will depend on the manner in which the child understands her. If the child doesn't really know its mother and expects from her a love that she isn't able to give, or a leniency that she knows isn't good for the child, this may well lead to doubts and frustrations that may last a lifetime.

Likewise, in order to believe in God—to trust in God—one must believe that God exists; but this isn't enough. One also needs to know God, to know that God is good, powerful, and loving. Only when one knows this will one's trust in God lead to doing the will of God. A misguided "believing that" which sees in God only a vengeful judge will lead to an embittered faith that understands its task as simply judging others as harshly as possible. The mother-and-child comparison again applies. When the child grows in age, it also grows in its understanding of its mother, and its trust in her will be more solidly grounded as the child discovers what may be expected of her and what not. So also, as believers come to a better understanding of God, our faith and trust in God will be closer to the mark.

Therefore, "believing that" and "believing in" are interconnected: "believing that" improves and strengthens our "believing in," and in turn our "believing in" also improves and strengthens our "believing that." In other words, the more we understand God, the better we will be able to trust and rest in God. And the more we trust in God, the better we will understand God.

## Understanding Doctrine

In a way, the relationship between "believing in" and "believing that" is parallel to the manner in which faith relates to doctrine. Faith is an attitude of trust in God, while doctrines are ideas or positions that we hold. Faith saves; doctrines do not. Doctrines by themselves can lead to convictions and beliefs, but not to faith. Faith is a relationship with God; doctrines tell us about God.

Just as "believing in" requires a measure of "believing that," so true faith is expressed in doctrines that help us understand and clarify the nature of this God in whom we believe, and thus help us avoid confusing the true God with any of the many idols of the world.

At this point it is necessary to clarify the nature and function of doctrine. Today there are many who wish to have nothing to do with religious doctrines. This is quite understandable in view of the manner in which doctrines have often been employed. Sometimes they are wielded as weapons to force everybody to agree on all things. But that isn't the true or the proper function of doctrines.

In order to clarify the purpose of doctrines and their function, an example may be in order. Suppose that we all live on a high, wide, and fertile plateau, surrounded by cliffs. On that plateau we can all move with freedom. Some prefer one area to another; some seek shadows, while others seek sun. The beauty of the plateau itself impels us to explore it, to learn about it all we can. But one day an explorer comes so close to the edge that the stone on which he stands collapses, and he falls down the cliff. In light of this tragedy, we who live on the plateau build a fence to warn others of the danger in that area. But then comes the day when a similar tragedy occurs at the other end of the same plateau. In response, we build another fence there, as a warning against hidden dangers. The purpose of such fences isn't to limit the freedom of the inhabitants of the plateau, but exactly the opposite. By warning us about the dangerous areas into which it is perilous to venture, those fences give us the freedom we need to move across various areas of the plateau without fear, and to be creative about what we do on the plateau.

This is the proper function of doctrines. When properly understood and employed, doctrines don't try to tell us exactly what we ought to believe. Instead, their purpose is to warn us about some of the tenets and beliefs that may well be like cliffs that take us beyond the safe limits of the plateau of faith. Throughout this book we will see many cases in which this is true. For the present, we may take one by way of example: the person of Jesus Christ. In the past there were some who so much sought to exalt him and his divinity that they turned him into a phantom that wasn't truly human. Against such opinions, others built fences affirming the true humanity of the Savior. At the other extreme were others who so underscored the humanity of Jesus that they denied his divinity. This also led to the building of fences affirming that divinity. By using this example, I don't mean to suggest that we all have to understand Jesus in the same manner. Just as on our hypothetical plateau, where some people prefer the shade and others seek the sun, so in the church there will always be some people who emphasize the humanity of Jesus, and others who underscore his divinity. They can do this with greater freedom and security precisely because there are doctrinal fences that warn them about the cliffs at each of the extremes.

In passing, this means that we have to think again about those whom we call "heretics." The famous heretics that have appeared at various stages in the history of the church—particularly during its first few centuries—weren't evil people seeking to twist the faith and to lead others astray. They were explorers who were so interested in knowing the plateau that they fell into error. It was precisely such experiences that then led the church to formulate doctrines—to build fences—that would warn believers of the dangers at various places.

In summary, doctrines are good and necessary. But one must also be aware of the manner in which they are so often misused. There are those who, rather than employing doctrines in order to let us know about possible cliffs that may threaten our faith, employ them in order to force us all to think in exactly the same way. What happens in such cases is that new and unnecessary fences are built away from the edges and closer and closer to interior parts of the plateau, so that there will be less and less freedom to explore. We wish to dot all the i's and cross all the t's, as if we were truly able to circumscribe and describe God. And so the fences, rather than functioning as warnings to prevent dangerous missteps, become herding pens in which we are all forced into the same opinions. It is precisely this wrongful and even abusive use of doctrines that has given them a bad name, leading many to consider doctrines restrictive.

So, what this book seeks to do is to explain something about the main doctrines of Christianity. Its purpose is not to make us all agree on everything. Rather, its goal is to help us to understand the common faith of all these various people who dwell together on this high plateau of faith where God has placed us through the work of the Holy Spirit. This will help us not only to celebrate and experience that common faith, but also to understand and to accept those other sisters and brothers in the faith with whom we differ on some particular point—or, continuing our earlier metaphor, those who live in a different zone of the plateau.

Now, in the spirit of prayer and mutual love, let us move into the study of some of the main doctrines of Christianity.

## For Reflection and Discussion

1. Suppose that a devout young student tells you that he or she has decided not to go into advanced studies, or that someone is telling young people in the church that they shouldn't go to college or study science, because that will destroy their faith. What can we say to such a person? What reasons would someone have for believing that study destroys faith?

2. Is it helpful to think about doctrines as fences warning us of dangers? Is it true that when used in this manner, doctrines actually give us more freedom rather than forcing us all to think in a particular way?

3. What fences or doctrines do we consider absolutely necessary? In other words, what doctrines are essential to Christian faith? Make a list of them. In future chapters we'll probably be discussing some of them. As you move further in this study, look again at that list and see what you might add or subtract.

4. Suppose that someone tells you that, since the Bible speaks of bishops, bishops are necessary, and someone else tells you that, since in ancient times the church in each city governed itself, congregational government is the only one that's valid. Are those differences in belief sufficient for them to reject one another? Are they sufficient for you to reject them? What other similar differences stand between us? What can we do about them?

5. What do you think are the most serious "cliffs"—false doctrines—threatening the church today? Again, you may wish to make a list of these and reconsider it as you read the rest of this book.

*[Handwritten margin notes:]*

gospel of prosperity

wrapping religion in flag

christian nationalist

- God isn't protector of faith

back burner

cold storage - things you don't understand yet

accept

*necessary doctrines*

1- Christ Jesus / incarnate / revelation of God

2- God fully human / fully God

3 Holy Spirit

4. Jesus example of how to live w/ God + each other

5- Church / Community / body of Christ / accountability (personal)

6- Welcome - those outside fences

Church Government

Hierarchal
Episcopal
Catholic
Orthodox
Anglican
methodist
AME

Presby
Authority Elder
Connection Presbytery
Presbyterian
Reformed

# ONE

# *Revelation*

When speaking about God, the first thing we have to say is that the only way to know God is through God's own disclosure. This doesn't mean that in order to know something about God one has to have a special revelation. But it does mean that our knowledge of God depends on what God wishes us to know. It's a matter not of our discovering God, but rather of a God who uncovers Godself to us. If, for instance, we say that we discovered God by looking at nature, this isn't due to our particular perspicacity, but rather to God being willing to be revealed in nature. The same is true if we say that we see God in the person of Jesus, or in Scripture, or in our personal experience. In order for us really to encounter God through any of these means, first of all it is necessary for God to wish to be known through them.

The second thing one must say regarding this matter is that God's revelation is always adapted to our capacity to understand and know God's nature. The absolute knowledge of God is not within our reach as mortals. As God says to Moses,

"No one shall see me and live" (Exod. 33:20). Thus, revelation itself is a sign of God's grace. Out of love God makes Godself known to us and, also out of love, adapts revelation to our capacity to receive it.

Some examples taken from sports and from education may help us understand this. In baseball, if there were ever a pitcher who could throw a ball at 500 mph, that wouldn't be particularly useful, because there is no catcher able to catch such a ball. In education, a teacher with a PhD in mathematics teaching first-grade children cannot teach them trigonometry or calculus. Both the pitching and the teaching have to adapt themselves to the capabilities of those receiving them. Likewise, God's revelation is adapted to our capability of receiving it. God's revelation is the result of a God who so loved us as to adapt to our condition, coming to us first in the written Word, and then in the Word made flesh. "For God so loved the world . . ."

## God in Nature and in History

Where and how is God revealed? Perhaps on this score we must begin by affirming that God is revealed first of all in the emptiness of our hearts. No matter what religion or philosophy we follow, we all know that we are incomplete beings. Not only is the universe a mystery, but so is life itself. Both those who flee from religion and those who embrace it know in the depth of their souls that they need a point of reference outside themselves. As Augustine says at the very beginning of his *Confessions,* "You have made us for yourself, and our hearts are restless until they come to rest in you."

If we then look around with the openness resulting from acknowledging our own incompleteness, the first thing we can say is that we see God in nature. As the psalmist says, "The heavens are telling the glory of God; and the firmament proclaims his handiwork" (Ps. 19:1). And the apostle Paul echoes that information: "Ever since the creation of the world his eternal power and divine nature, invisible though they are, have been understood and seen through the things he has made" (Rom. 1:20). One doesn't have to be a poet or a visionary in order to be overwhelmed by the mysteries of subatomic particles or the vastness of interstellar space, and even more so by our inability to comprehend such things. As the psalmist says, "When I look at your heavens, the work of your fingers, the moon and the stars that you have established; what are human beings that you are mindful of them, mortals that you care for them?" (Ps. 8:3–4).

As we see God in nature, we begin to discover God's infinite wisdom. The more we explore the functioning of nature, the more surprised we are at the wisdom of its creator. If the psalmist was overwhelmed by the movement of the heavenly bodies, much more overwhelmed are we today as scientists discover more about those very bodies, about atoms and their minuscule particles, or the manner in which a single cell carries within itself an entire code of reproduction. But above all, the contemplation of nature, as in the case of the psalmist, lets us see the enormous gulf between God's wisdom and ours. Paradoxically, the more we study nature and the better we understand it, the more aware we are of how little we really understand.

Sometimes we are attracted by the serene beauty of nature, and at other points by its majestic power. Sometimes as we look at nature we're soothed by the calm beauty of a pool in a small river, and sometimes we're overwhelmed by the irrepressible might of a waterfall. We see the power and wisdom of God both in the afternoon breeze and in the raging tempest.

But nature alone does not suffice. While the contemplation of nature may prove inspiring, it is also perplexing. In nature there is not only life, harmony, and beauty, but also death, corruption, ugliness, and violence. Thus nature points us towards the great mystery of God; but by itself it can never tell us much about the will of that God. Therefore, in order to understand nature in such a way that we can discern the presence of God in it, we need a further guide that is not nature itself.

This is why ancient Israel, surrounded by peoples who worshiped gods and goddesses of nature, always insisted that its God is not only the Lord of nature, but also the Lord of history. The God of Israel not only made the heavens and the earth, but also intervened with a mighty arm in order to free the children of Israel from the yoke of Egypt. Both Judaism and Christianity are based on the premise that God is always present and active in history. God is not a distant being who sets the world going and then abandons it. Thus, by studying history one can begin to discern the divine action in it. And this is true not only of the history that we study at school, which deals with empires and invasions, but also with that other but perhaps more important history that is each of our lives, as well as the history of the church itself.

But even history, like nature, includes much that we certainly cannot attribute to God. History includes a long series of abuses, violent conquests, and genocides. And even where things don't go that far, there are also corrupt governments and demagogues who abuse their power. Furthermore, as we study history, we see that the church itself is not exempt from crime and abuse. And our own personal history also includes its high points and its lows—times in which we have seen the hand of God as well as times of anxiety, perplexity, and infidelity. Therefore, in order to understand all those various levels of history in such a way that we can discern the presence of God in them, we need another guide that is not history itself.

We Christians are convinced that such a guide is to be found in the Scriptures, where the people of Israel discern and celebrate the presence of God in their own history at the same time that the prophets call them to repentance for their own faithlessness and disobedience. In Scripture, God lets us see the divine action in our human past, and on that basis calls us to discern the divine presence in our present history so as to be faithful and obedient.

But there is more. Our God speaks to us not only in nature and in history, and not only in the history of Israel as explained in the writings of the biblical prophets. Ours is a God who in Jesus Christ has become part of nature and of history in order to be known by us. Further on, in a later chapter, we will deal more extensively with the person of Jesus Christ. For the time being, the words of the book of

Hebrews immediately come to mind: "Long ago God spoke to our ancestors in many and various ways by the prophets, but in these last days he has spoken to us by a Son, whom he appointed heir of all things, through whom he also created the worlds. He is a reflection of God's glory and the exact imprint of God's very being, and he sustains all things by his powerful word" (Heb. 1:1–3).

## How Does Scripture Reveal God?

Since in another chapter we will return to the subject of God's revelation and action in Jesus Christ, here we must take the time to consider Scripture and its interpretation. On this matter, one must begin by affirming that the interpretation of Scripture requires the intervention of the Holy Spirit. In the past there has been much discussion about how the Holy Spirit inspired the authors of Scripture. Although there are significant differences regarding the manner in which that inspiration works, in general believers agree that Scripture is the Word of God by reason of the inspiration of the Holy Spirit. What we often forget is that this inspiration isn't limited to the time when the text was written, but also takes place when it is read and interpreted. Without the Holy Spirit, it's possible to read the Bible simply as a collection of ancient literary pieces, some more elegant than others, which one approaches with the same curiosity and the same methods that one employs, for instance, in reading the writings of Plato. Furthermore, in the church itself there have been believers who have employed the Bible in order to condemn those who are not like them, to justify injustice and oppression, and even to do violence to their enemies. For the Bible to be the Word of God for us, it is necessary that in our own reading and interpretation the Holy Spirit be at work.

And we need to consider other points besides this one. The first is that the Bible is a revelation, and not a sort of puzzle that God has given us awaiting the arrival of some supposed prophet who knows how to solve it. Looking for a "secret key" or a mystical number that would allow us to understand the entirety of biblical history is to deny the very nature of Scripture as the revelation of God—of a God who out of love reveals Godself to us, and who in this process doesn't present us with puzzles to solve and certainly doesn't play silly games with us.

Second, if God has given us Scripture as well as the means to understand whatever we see and read, it behooves us to employ those means in our reading of Scripture. It's not simply a matter of asking the Holy Spirit to inspire us in the reading—that's absolutely necessary. But that same Holy Spirit gives us the numerous resources that we must also consider and use. These resources include, among other things, translations that allow us to read the text in our own language. Without such translations, most of us would be at a loss, unable to understand a single word of the sacred texts. There's no doubt that those who gave us those translations invoked the help of the Holy Spirit for their work. Some of them risked freedom and life in that enterprise, and for that we must be profoundly grateful. But the fact that the Holy Spirit accompanied them in their task as translators doesn't mean that they were infallible. In English, every version has been revised once and again as we've developed better knowledge of the original languages and found better ancient manuscripts, and also as the English language itself has evolved.

This means that our various interpretations of Scripture, even though they're guided by the Holy Spirit, are not infallible. They frequently need correction, just as the ancient versions of the Bible do. This is of great importance, because if we forget it, we may fall into the trap of thinking that if our interpretation is correct, then it must be seen as infallible, and that if at some point we err, this implies that the Holy Spirit didn't accompany us in our reading. In truth, even when the Holy Spirit inspires our reading, all our interpretations of Scripture are *ours*, and therefore are subject to correction.

This constant need for correction is one of the reasons why one must underline the importance of reading Scripture within the context of the community. One must certainly develop the discipline of reading the Bible and meditating on it in private. This has become much easier in the last several centuries thanks to the invention of the printing press, which allows us to have Bibles in our own homes. But that private reading must not take the place of the study of Scripture in community. If we stop to think about it, we will realize that almost all of the Bible was written in order to be read in public: the Old Testament, to be read before the congregation of Israel; and the New, to be read out loud in the church. The Old Testament isn't addressed to individual Israelites, and the New Testament isn't addressed primarily to the individual believer. Even though our own personal faith is of great importance, the purpose of the Bible is not only our individual formation, but is also and above all the formation and guidance of the people of God. When, for instance, Paul writes to believers in Rome, he's taking for granted that his epistle will be read out loud in the presence of the entire congregation. Naturally, some of the people who were present at that point would later wish to read it again with more care. (But during these times there were no printed books, and therefore it would have been very difficult for an individual believer to have even a portion of the Bible at home.) Both elements—community reading and private reading—are necessary. In our case, the community of faith helps us to discern between what is truly inspired by the Holy Spirit and what is nothing more than our personal opinion.

But it's not enough to read within the closely knit community of faith with which we gather periodically. Such reading is very important, because it is within that community that our faith is shaped and nourished. But we must remember first of all that just as we are reading and interpreting Scripture, millions of sisters and brothers throughout the whole world are also reading and interpreting it. In whatever measure we can, we must take their perspectives into account, for all of these people are part of the same body of Christ to which we belong. For instance, it's easy for a local congregation in the United States whose members are mostly of European descent to celebrate Thanksgiving by thanking God for "this land you gave us." But it becomes much more difficult to say the same words if we consider ourselves to be in the presence of brothers and sisters who descend from the original inhabitants of these lands, and who still remember that their ancestors were dispossessed of them by force.

Furthermore, it doesn't suffice to remember those others who today walk in a spiritual pilgrimage that is also ours. We must also recall the enormous cloud of witnesses who have walked before us and in whose steps we now follow. The Bible itself has come to us thanks to many generations of people who carefully copied and recopied it when there was no printing press. It has come to us through many generations of people who devotedly studied the original languages of the sacred text so that we might receive it in a way that we can understand. It has come to us through a long chain of believers throughout the centuries. All of these people are also part of our community of faith, and we must take all of them into account in our study of Scripture.

We see some of that in the Bible itself. The prophets of the Bible don't speak as if Abraham and Moses had never existed. The Psalms are inspired by the stories of Abraham, Moses, and the prophets. The New Testament opens with the genealogy that relates the story of Jesus with the entire history of Israel. And Jesus himself reminds us of all this when he says that our God, the God of Abraham, Sarah, and their descendants "is God not of the dead, but of the living" (Matt. 22:32).

This is why, as we are often told, the first principle of biblical interpretation is that the sacred text is to be interpreted in the light of the Bible itself. It's not just that the Bible doesn't contradict itself, but really that the Bible tells us the history of the relationship between God and the people of God—Israel and the church. Just as the authors of the Gospels read the entire history of Israel and the beginnings of the church as a single history, so today we must read the entire biblical text as a single history—our history as God's people.

## How Scripture Interprets Us

What is most important in all this is that this history is our history. No matter how distant in time, it is not far from our own story. On the contrary, it is the story that makes us who we are, that defines us. And this means that ultimately it is not enough to interpret Scripture, but it is also necessary—and perhaps even more important—that Scripture interprets us.

This probably needs a bit of explanation. Too often we read and interpret Scripture with an attitude that is guided mostly by curiosity. We want to know how things are—even how many angels there are, and how many different kinds and ranks are mentioned. We want to determine the date of the second coming of the Lord. But we must ask ourselves if such curiosity may not well be a way of evading obedience. As we spend time investigating and discussing such matters, we may forget the central fact that the Bible exists primarily not to satisfy our curiosity, but rather to guide us and call us into obedience and hope.

In fact, what is most important is not to know what the Bible says in general, but rather to know, understand, and obey what the Bible tells us today in our concrete situation, particularly those matters involving commands that we would rather not have to obey. In a word, one may know the Bible quite thoroughly and not be biblical. The Bible is well known by those who can repeatedly quote verses on any given subject, and who can even recite entire chapters by heart. But if someone, even knowing all that, spends time gossiping and backbiting, or promotes divisions in the church, or takes advantage of those who are weaker, he or she is not truly a biblical person. And the same is true of the church. A local congregation is not more biblical because it reads the Bible more—even though we all need to read the Bible. A church is truly biblical when biblical love is practiced and shown in it—when in it one experiences the grace of God; when it is concerned for the poor and the afflicted; when in it one catches a glimpse of the promised reign of God.

This may be stated otherwise: our main purpose in reading the Bible must not be information, but rather formation. When we read, for instance, the story of Abraham, what is important is not that we learn by heart the entire route of his pilgrimage, but rather that somehow we come to share that faith which guided him throughout his journey.

*　　　*　　　*

Let's summarize what has been said thus far. We are able to know God because God wills it to be so and therefore reveals Godself to us. That revelation may be seen in nature and in history. Scripture is the Word of God because it witnesses to God's activity in the history of the people of God (and because, as we shall see in another chapter, it witnesses to Jesus Christ and thus allows us to know something about this God who "so loved the world"). Since the purpose of Scripture is to shape and lead the people of God, our reading must have a communal dimension. And, finally, we should read the Bible not primarily to satisfy our curiosity, but rather to be called to obedience within a disobedient world, and to hope in a world that wallows in despair.

## For Reflection and Discussion

1. Think back to times when you've felt that you were in particularly close communion with God. If you're studying this book with a group, share those experiences. Among all those moments, how many involve seeing God in nature, how many in history, and how many in Scripture?

2. There is a well-known hymn about God's presence in creation:

> This is my Father's world,
> and to my listening ears
> all nature sings, and round me rings
> the music of the spheres.

> This is my Father's world:
> I rest me in the thought
> of rocks and trees, of skies and seas—
> His hands the wonders wrought.

This is my Father's world:
the birds their carols raise;
the morning light, the lily white,
declare their Maker's praise.

This is my Father's world:
he shines in all that's fair;
in the rustling grass I hear Him pass.
He speaks to me everywhere.

Can you think of moments when you felt that these words expressed your feelings and experience? Can you think of other moments when your experience of nature didn't quite agree with this hymn?

3. Review your own story. Where in it can you see the hand of God? What have your various experiences taught you about God?

4. Review the background of your story, or of the group's story. How did you come to faith? Who are your ancestors in the faith? Although they weren't perfect, how did God use them to lead you to faith?

5. Think about these questions and discuss them with others: What is your favorite part of the Bible? (This could be an entire book or a particular passage.) Why is this your favorite? What is the place of this particular passage or book in the entire history of the people of God that the Bible recounts?

# TWO

# The Triune Creator God

Throughout history, countless numbers have sought and offered proofs of God's existence. Most of these proofs are based on the world that we see around us: its complexity requires the existence of a wise Creator. One of these proofs uses the example of a watch found in the middle of the desert, which is a certain indication that somebody has put it there. Other more abstract and complex proofs are grounded in philosophical reasoning that we need not repeat here. In any case, the truth is that any "proof" of the existence of God offers no more than a distant glimpse of the God in whom Christians believe. After all, any god that our minds are able to comprehend and demonstrate isn't the true sovereign God of Christian faith. All of our proofs, or speculations, or other ideas about God still fall far short of the reality of this God whom we experience and in whose hands we trust our very existence.

This is true, and yet the first thing that Christian faith affirms regarding this God, whom our words can never describe nor our minds understand, is that God is love. As the Psalms repeatedly say, "his mercy endures forever." Using more abstract words, sometimes we say that God is "immutable." But by this we don't mean that God is insensible, like a stone or a piece of firewood. On the contrary, God's immutability refers to God's constant loving presence on which we can always count, no matter what. This is why the Bible often refers to God as a father. The immutability of our Parent God does not imply insensibility but exactly the opposite: the thing that does not change in a good parent, no matter the circumstances, is love.

Another fundamental assertion of Christianity is that God is the creator of all that exists. When in the early church a person was about to be baptized, the first question posed was this: "Do you believe in God the Father Almighty, maker of heaven and earth?" (Or, in another formula, "maker of all things visible and invisible.")

## Understanding the Doctrine of Creation

In recent times the doctrine of creation has been a subject of much controversy. If some scientists speak of an evolution that has taken millions of years and that hasn't been guided by the hand of a creator, but is rather a matter of chance, are they right? When others speak about a creation that took six days, are they right? When the issues are posed in this manner, we must simply say that both err.

On the one hand, it is quite possible for scientists to show that millions of years ago, before there were any human beings, dinosaurs walked on the earth. They can also show the relationship between the various species of plants and animals, and how they have evolved. But they will never be able to prove that all this, or the origin of humankind, is only the result of a series of coincidences or accidents without any particular direction. When scientists make such a claim, they have gone beyond the limits of what scientific methods can prove, and are simply speculating. Their claim is not a properly scientific one.

On the other hand, those who insist that the world was created in six days, and that this is the meaning of the doctrine of creation, should probably go back and read the Bible again. It's clear that at the beginning of Genesis there are two stories of creation that coincide in their theological meaning, but not in matters such as the order of the creation of things. In chapter 1 we hear of the six days of creation. In this story, the last thing that God makes, after all the animals, is human beings, man and woman at the same time. But in chapter 2, there is no word about the six days of creation, and there's a different order. In this story, God creates first the man and then the animals to serve him as company, and finally the woman, who is to be the man's perfect companion. It will not do to claim that one of these stories is correct and the other isn't. Nor should we, as many have done, take a bit from each of the two stories, forget what doesn't fit our scheme, and then call this "the biblical account of creation." What we really must do is to discern the teaching or central message of both stories, the teaching on which both agree. When we follow this path, we see that both stories categorically affirm that all that exists is created by God. It is not the case that some things are made by God and others by an evil spirit or a lesser god. And since God is good, all that exists is good. This is particularly underscored with a repetition in the first story: every time God finishes something, we are told that "God saw that it was good."

This was the point that was always emphasized by the ancient church when they spoke about creation. It wasn't a matter of explaining the origin of all things, or giving a detailed account of how they were made. Instead, it was a matter of affirming that all that exists is the work of God. Everything that exists is part of God's good creation, even though our misuse can corrupt it. This is why the first question posed to a person about to be baptized was whether he or she believed in this God Father, maker of all things, visible and invisible. This question obviously had to do with God the creator, but it also had important implications for the manner in which one saw the world that God has created.

This means that there is a close relationship between the doctrine of creation and the basic affirmation that ours is a God of love. When we speak of the love of God as that of a father, we frequently remember that a father protects and finds nourishment for his children. There's no doubt that this is part of what we mean when we say that God is our parent. But we must remember another dimension of parental or maternal love: when a responsible couple decides to have a child, they know full well that at some point the child will assert its own independence, perhaps get into difficult situations, and quite possibly break their hearts. They may well have many dreams and purposes for this new person, but they know that this child will not be the same as they are, and may seek out different dreams and purposes. When God decides to create the universe, God does this out of a similar love, even knowing that these creatures will rebel and will break God's heart. Even so, by reason of that immense love, God has created us, as well as all that we see around us.

In brief, the doctrine of creation affirms that all that exists is the work of a God of love, and that therefore those of us who claim God as our parent have to love this creation that God has placed around us. And it also affirms that, just like an earthly parent, God has given a measure of independence to this creation—and, as we shall see in the following chapter, particularly to humankind—so that it is able to determine its own course. All of this is one more sign of the fundamental Christian assertion that God is love.

Therefore, when we say that creation is the result of God's love, we are also affirming that, as those who seek to serve and obey this God, we must also build our lives and our relationships on love. This includes both our interpersonal relationships and the manner in which we relate to the rest of this beautiful creation of God.

But we must also remember that even the word "love," rather than an exact description of who and how God is, is a sign or an analogy pointing to God's reality. In our human experience, there is nothing higher than love. When we say that God is love, we're saying that the best way to understand God is through our human experience of love. But we must still remember that divine love is far above any human love. In our experience, love is often the opposite of justice. Thus, for instance, if we forgive someone, we say that we do it out of love; and if we punish someone, we say that we do it for the sake of justice. This has led some people to think that sometimes God acts out of love and sometimes out of justice. Some have even said that when God saves someone, God does so out of love, and that when someone is condemned to eternal punishment, this is done out of justice. This contrast between love and justice led some in ancient times to think that there are two gods, one loving and the other demanding justice, and to say that, while the New Testament speaks of the former, the Old Testament refers to the latter. (In the second century, such were the teachings of Marcion, which the church rejected. The article on creation in the Apostles' Creed, which wasn't written by the apostles but was created in the early church as a short statement of apostolic teaching for use in teaching and worship, seems designed at least in part to set up a fence preventing others from falling into this error.)

Such teachings simply aren't true. In both Testaments God is seen as a God of justice and of love. It's better to say that God's love is so vast that it comes to be the same as justice. Or, to say the same thing in a different way, that God's justice is so different from human justice that it is a justice of love. This was the famous discovery of Martin Luther that freed him from a condition that, as he himself would later say, made it impossible for him to love God. His discovery was that when Paul referred to "the justice of God" in Romans, he was speaking of a divine love of such magnitude that God declares us to be just even while we are sinners. At any rate, in a manner that we do not understand, God always acts justly, and at the same time God always acts lovingly.

But to claim that "God is love" implies much more. It also implies that we have to understand God in a very particular way. This is the ultimate reason for the doctrine of the Trinity, which most Christians accept and follow. That doctrine has created serious difficulties throughout the history of the church, and still does, partly because we don't explain it clearly. For that reason, it's a good idea to take a moment to look at it more carefully.

### Understanding the Doctrine of the Trinity

The very foundation of the doctrine of the Trinity is to be found in the Bible, where we see that Jesus is divine, but is not to be confused with the Father. And, likewise, it is clear that the Holy Spirit is also divine, but is not to be confused with Jesus or with the Father. The Bible affirms that God was made flesh in Jesus Christ. At the very beginning of the Gospel of John, we read that the Word was God and was with God, and that this Word "became flesh and lived among us" (John 1:14). But that same Gospel clearly distinguishes between Jesus and the Father, so that on the one hand Jesus claims that whoever has seen him has seen the Father (14:9), but on the other hand says that he will "ask the Father" (14:16). The same is true for the Holy Spirit, whom Jesus, in the just-quoted verse, calls "another Advocate." And then, in the next chapter of this Gospel, we see a clear distinction between the Advocate, the Father, and Jesus: "When the Advocate comes, whom I will send to you from the Father, the Spirit of truth who comes from the Father, he will testify on my behalf" (15:26).

Throughout history, Christians have constantly debated the exact meaning of this. In those debates we see another example of what we discussed earlier about the function of doctrines. Among those who have affirmed the Trinity in past centuries, some have stressed God's unity, while others have emphasized the distinction among the three divine persons—the Father, the Son, and the Holy Spirit. Despite such differences, they are all considered orthodox, as long as they do not stress the unity of the Godhead to such a point that they forget the distinction among the three persons, or stress that distinction to the point that they seem to be speaking of three gods. The doctrine of the Trinity is like the fences at the edge of the plateau that we discussed in the last chapter: on the one hand, this doctrine prevents us from believing in three gods, and on the other hand, it reminds us that we must not confuse the three persons.

Throughout history, many different illustrations, examples, and metaphors have been offered in order to express the doctrine of the Trinity. Possibly there is no better illustration or explanation of the Trinity than that of Augustine. He points out that in our mind there is memory, will, and reason. Memory is not the same as will, nor is it the same as reason. But the three are a single mind. Furthermore, one cannot say that the mind has three different parts. In a way, the entire mind is memory, the entire mind is will, and the entire mind is reason. When our will decides to do something, it does this on the basis of what memory and reason tell it—although, obviously, the human mind may go astray in its will, as well as in its memory and in its reasoning. The unity within the Godhead among the Father, the Son, and the Holy Spirit is similar to that which exists in the human mind.

Such examples or illustrations are helpful. But perhaps rather than approaching the doctrine of the Trinity as if it were a puzzle or an insoluble contradiction, we should look at it as a way of understanding what is meant when we declare at the same time that God is one and that God is love. When we say that God is love, we are affirming not only that God loves us or that God loves all of creation, but also that within the very Godhead there is love. God loves Godself. God doesn't wait to create other beings in order to love. The doctrine of the Trinity affirms that the unity of God is very different from what we commonly understand as being one. Being one shouldn't make us think that God is a monolith, impassible, unable to relate to others—not even within Godself. Being one in the sense in which God is one is relating to oneself in such a way that there is love within one's unity. The love among the Father, the Son, and the Holy Spirit is such that the three are one. The importance of love is such that within the very Godhead there is a dynamic of love.

All of this may seem like unimportant speculation, but the truth is that it has much to tell us about our own reality. The God who is never alone, the God in whose bosom there is love, is the same one who in Genesis 2:18 declares that "it is not good for the man to be alone." The God in whose inner being there is a harmonious diversity is the God in whose creation all things are mutually related. In past centuries, our ancestors in the faith referred to this as the "vestiges of the Trinity in its creatures." But such vestiges are to be found not only in each creature individually considered; they exist also and above all in the manner in which all of God's creatures are interconnected. In a way, this complex creation is a single one. We need not go much further than considering the law of gravity. According to that law, not only does the earth attract all that is on its surface, but all matter, even the smallest and the most distant, attracts all other matter. Creation is one in a manner similar to that in which God is one and at the same time triune.

*　　*　　*

Like every other doctrine, the doctrines of creation and of the Trinity have important practical consequences for our lives as believers. The doctrine of creation, which too often we limit to discussions and theories about beginnings, is a sign of the way in which we are to relate to everything around us. The Trinity, which we often consider an enigma to be solved, or even an irrelevant rhetoric of times past, is to be seen as an example to imitate. Just as God is one because God is love, so are we humans called to be one in love. We will talk more about this in the following chapter.

## For Reflection and Discussion

1. Is it possible to prove the existence of God? What arguments can we offer to that effect? Is it true that any god whose existence the human mind can prove falls far short of the God of our faith?

2. Considering the questions above, of what use are the many proofs and arguments that are frequently used to affirm the existence of God? Can such arguments lead us to believe in the God and Father of Jesus Christ? Or is their function to remove obstacles that may keep us or others away from faith?

3. Is it true that scientists are unable to prove by a purely scientific method that the universe and life in it are the result of a series of random coincidences?

4. Take your Bible and compare the two stories of creation that appear in the first two chapters of Genesis. What are their common points? How do the two stories differ?

5. In our daily life, does it make any difference whether or not we believe in the doctrine of creation?

6. Do you see a relationship between the declaration that God is love and the doctrine of the Trinity? What difference does it make today whether we believe in the Trinity or not? What difference does it make for the manner in which we relate to others?

# THREE

# *Humankind*

The psalmist asked God, "What are human beings that you are mindful of them, mortals that you care for them?" (Ps. 8:4). The Bible gives us a clear answer: humans are important because they are the work of this God of whom the same psalm says, "I look at your heavens, the work of your fingers, the moon and the stars that you established." Furthermore, human beings are not just part of creation, but in some ways its high point. Once again we may quote the same psalm: "You have made them a little lower than God, and crowned them with glory and honor. You gave them dominion over the works of your hands."

This may be seen also in the two stories of creation in Genesis. In the first of these, after creating the sun and the moon, as well as all the animals, God creates human beings, male and female at the same time, and gives them "dominion over the fish of the sea, and over the birds of the air, and over the cattle, and over all the wild animals of the earth, and every creeping thing that creeps upon the earth"

(Gen. 1:26). In the second story, God creates first the male and a garden in which he is to dwell. Then God makes the animals that will keep the man company, and brings them before him so that he may name them. In the Hebrew tradition, as in many ancient cultures, the authority to name was a sign of authority over the named.

Both stories in Genesis point out that God has placed human beings on earth with certain responsibilities. In Genesis 1, God tells the first human couple that they are to fill the earth and subdue it (Gen. 1:28). In Genesis 2, we are told that God placed the man in the garden "to till it and keep it" (Gen. 2:15). In other words, although we often think otherwise, these stories don't tell us that God created the earth as it was intended to be in the end, as if it were a finished thing. Rather, they tell us that God placed human beings on earth to take it along the paths that God wished, to till and keep it, to rule it as God's representatives. This is what we often call "stewardship," to which we will return later on.

At this juncture it's important to point out that we were not given lordship over creation so that we might exploit it and destroy it. Throughout history there has been much discussion about the nature of the likeness of God that, according to Genesis, we carry. Some have used this to claim that God has a human shape—a point which needs no further discussion. What is clear in Genesis 1:26 is that a close relationship exists between the image of God in humankind and human lordship over creation. Just as God is Lord over all creation, so this human being, in the likeness of God, has a parallel lordship. This lordship, however, is after the image of the likeness of God, who is a God of love, a God who precisely out of that love allows us sufficient freedom even to be disobedient. Therefore, when properly understood, human lordship over creation gives us no right to do with it as we please, but rather provides us the opportunity and the obligation to use and guide it just as a father and a mother guide their children, or as God guides us: with love and freedom.

## Created for Connection and Love

Human beings have been created to live in community—meaning community with the rest of creation, but also the higher sense of community with other humans. In the first story in Genesis, humankind is a couple from the very moment of its creation. In the second story, where God creates the male first, God declares that "it is not good that the man should be alone; I will make him a helper as his partner" (Gen. 2:18).

It may be worthwhile to stop here to say a word about this notion of "a helper as his partner." This has frequently been understood to mean that the function of the woman is to help the man as a subordinate being. But the Hebrew words behind this passage have a very different sense. The word "helper" employed here is frequently applied in the Old Testament to God, who is Israel's helper. And what is translated as a "partner" is similar to the image in a mirror. Unfortunately, in English, these two words were originally translated in the old King James Version as "an help meet for him"—meaning "an appropriate help." But later these two words were combined into a new one, "helpmeet," and into this word were poured all our traditional views and prejudices regarding the role and subordination of women.

In the story itself we are told that God creates first the man, then the animals to keep him company, and finally the woman. Upon creating each animal, God brings it to the man so that he may name it and thus assume authority over it. But when God creates woman out of the rib of the man and brings her to him so that he may name her, the man acknowledges that this which is before him is flesh of his flesh and bone of his bone, and therefore, rather than giving her a name, he shares his name with her.

But the acknowledgment that it is not good for a human being to be alone is not to be limited to marriage or to being part of a couple; connection is part of the very essence of what it means to be human. A totally solitary and disconnected human being is not a full human being. What makes us who we are is above all a range of relationships with other people as well as with the rest of creation. If we are told, for instance, that a woman named Constance is a wife, a mother, a professor, and an astronomer, we are being told that she has a certain relationship with a particular man, with her children, with her students, with an academic institution, and probably even with the distant stars. Even her name tells us something about those who gave it to her and perhaps hints at the dreams and hopes they had for her. If we were told none of these things, we would know little about this person. It is all these relationships, and many more, that make her the person she is.

This is why many of the great teachers of Christian spirituality have come to the conclusion that one cannot be a Christian by oneself. In ancient times there were many who fled to a deserted place to live as solitary hermits, seeking to devote themselves to prayer and devotion and thus become better Christians. But in the end they discovered that to be true to their faith, they had to have other people around them whom they could love. Later, in the eighteenth century, John Wesley expressed this reality by saying that a "solitary saint" is a contradiction.

This could also be expressed in a different way: being made after the image of the triune God—of the God in whose very bosom love binds the three divine persons—means that we are made for love, and this truth is so fundamental that our own identity depends on whom and what we love, and how we love them. Being made after the image of God implies that we have been created for love and for loving in such a way and to such a degree that, bearing and showing the image of God, we may also lead lives of love.

### Created to Till and Be Tilled

The doctrine of creation tells us that all things are valuable and come from God. It also tells us much about who we are as human beings. There is no doubt that, as Genesis affirms, humankind was created by God as a species distinct from the other creatures. But what we often forget is that, according to Genesis 2, the beasts and the birds were made of the same dust of which we are made. Often, some in the church have tended to think that since we are spiritual beings, only that which is spiritual is important. But that is not so. No matter how much we may try to forget it, we are made of the same dirt as the eagle, the lion, and the worm. This isn't a bad thing, because it is the work of a God who at every step of creation declared that it was good. Thus, while we are unique beings within creation, we are also part of it. At the same time that our spirits dream of flying above the clouds, our bodies remind us that this is not all that we are.

In a way, what sets us apart from the rest of creation is that, besides our task of tilling and shaping the land, we also have the ability and the obligation to "till" ourselves— to shape our own lives. Of course there are limits beyond which we cannot go. Some of those limits are imposed on us by the society around us, and often result from the injustices within that society. Others are simply the result of having been made out of dirt like the eagle and the worm. Still, unlike the eagle and the worm, we have this unique ability to look at ourselves from the outside, to dream of what we are not, to give our lives a fresh shape. In short, in certain ways we have the capacity to create ourselves—or at least to shape ourselves—as a result of that which we believe, decide, and do. This is what is often meant by "free will." Within certain limits, we are able to shape our own lives, to create relationships that define us, to make decisions that determine much of what we will be.

This freedom, this possibility of looking at ourselves from the outside and deciding what we're going to do and who we're going to be, is simultaneously the most glorious and the most dangerous of the gifts that God has given us. Without it, we would be like the pebbles carried along by the river, or like the planets that simply revolve around the sun, or like the wolf pack that hunts because it's hungry. But it is this very freedom that has allowed us to disobey God, to poison the earth, and to give our lives a very different shape than what God intended. About fifteen hundred years ago, our brother Augustine said that this free will is an "intermediate good." What he meant by this is that freedom is a good gift from God. God has determined that we shall not be like the pebbles that move only when the current impels them; that we will have a measure of freedom to determine the course our lives will take and how we relate to the rest of creation. All of this is good. But because we can also use this freedom for evil and disobedience, it is an "intermediate good."

We may understand this better if we think in terms of parents and their child. The couple that decides to have a child knows that at some point this child, making use of its own freedom, will disobey them. Even so, they would much prefer a child who is able to disobey them than one who doesn't have such freedom. As parents, as we see our children grow, we frequently are disturbed by what they do or decide; but it would be tragic if they didn't have the freedom to do so.

Even though this might at first surprise us, such freedom implies a sort of absence. A good parent recognizes that for a child to grow and mature, she must be given her own space. As the child takes its first steps, a parent may worry that she might fall and hurt herself; but the parent also knows that if the child can constantly hold on to her parent's hands, she will never learn to walk. When the child becomes a teenager, the parent worries about the possibility that she may make serious mistakes—choosing bad company, experimenting with alcohol or drugs, being sexually irresponsible. But despite those risks, if the parent doesn't give the teenager a measure of freedom, she will never become a mature person. Thus, in a way, a parent must withdraw in order to give a child the necessary room to grow and develop.

As we read the story in Genesis 3, we might well ask, Where was God when the serpent tempted humans? Possibly the best way to begin understanding this is to think in terms of a parent who, precisely out of love, gives a child a certain space for the exercise of its freedom, even knowing the risk this involves.

## Created for Stewardship

We often use a biblical concept in other contexts that also helps us understand this matter of freedom: the idea of stewardship. When we speak in church about stewardship, we're usually referring to financial support for the church and its ministries, and probably also to the management of time, gifts, and so on. But stewardship is much more than that. In ancient times a steward was a person who managed the property of an owner who was sometimes absent. When the owner wasn't present or didn't intervene directly in the administration of the property, it was the task of the steward to do so in place of the owner, representing him. This meant that when the owner was present, the steward had to make every effort to learn about the owner's purposes and the way in which he wanted his property to be managed. But the real value of the steward was shown when the master was absent. Today we might say that something similar takes place in the relations between employees and a manager. Those employees who are faithful will seek to understand the purposes of the manager and what they themselves are expected to do. If the manager is good, employees will not be constantly watched and told what they have to do, but will have the freedom to deal with their responsibilities and to give periodic reports.

In the Gospels there are many parables that we usually call "parables of stewardship." It's interesting to note that in many of them the absence of the master is an important factor. In Matthew 25 we have the well-known parable of the ten talents, which begins by saying, "It is as if a man, going on a journey, summoned his slaves and entrusted his property to them. . . . Then he went away" (Matt. 25:14–15). In Mark 12, the parable of the wicked tenants tells of a man who planted and developed a vineyard and then "went to another country." In Luke 12, Jesus explains the responsibilities of a good steward: "Who then is the faithful and prudent manager whom his master will put in charge of his slaves, to give them their allowance of food at the proper time? Blessed is that slave whom his master will find at work when he arrives. Truly I tell you, he will put that one in charge of all his possessions. . . . [But] the slave who knew what his master wanted, but did not prepare himself or do what was wanted, will receive a severe beating" (Luke 12:42–44, 47). Further on, in chapter 19, the parable of the ten talents opens with "A nobleman went to a distant country. . . ." And in chapter 20 we find a variation of the beginning of Mark's parable about the wicked tenants: "A man planted a vine-yard . . . and went to another country for a long time." All of these parables deal with what a steward or a manager is to do while the master is absent.

Something similar happens in Genesis. According to the first of the two stories there, upon creating humankind after the divine image, God told them they were to rule over the fish of the ocean, the birds of the sky and the beasts, and over every animal that creeps on land. And in the second story God places humans in the Garden of Eden so that they may keep it and till it. God gives them instructions about what they are to do and what they are not to do. In other words, in both stories humankind receives authority over the rest of creation, in order to care for it or manage it according to the desires of the creator. So, from that very point of instruction, human beings are like stewards whom God has designated as managers of creation. God doesn't intend to manage creation directly, constantly intervening in every detail, or to supervise us in such a way as to deprive us of all freedom and responsibility.

So, when we speak of stewardship, we're dealing with more than how to manage the possessions or the time or the gifts we have. We're also speaking about how to use the power that God has given us over the rest of creation. And, given the complexity of society, which is a vast network of interrela-tionships, stewardship also implies that as managers we are responsible for others around us. Even though he doesn't like it and would deny it, Cain is responsible for his brother Abel.

When we come to the third chapter of Genesis, we see that humans have not been faithful stewards. God gave them power and instructions about how and within what limits to employ that power. But humans took the opportunity that freedom gave them in order to abuse their power and go beyond the limits established by God. God gave them both the freedom and the limits. But humans employed that freedom in order to ignore the limits.

This is what we usually call "the Fall." It's a story that depicts us just as we are. We all have a certain measure of freedom and of power. We know that while we have the right and the responsibility to make use of our freedom, we must not use it to abuse our power. That is the nature of sin. Sin is not only disobedience—it's an abuse of power, going beyond the limits that God has set. The story of Genesis takes place again and again in our lives and in our society. It is the story of a father who uses his power in order to force his son to be exactly as he wishes. It is the story of a young woman who uses her wiles and power of persuasion in order to get permission from her parents to do what she should not. It is the story of a politician who connives with an investor in order to exploit people. It is our human history, both individually and collectively.

This tragedy becomes even greater precisely because we are stewards. We've been given authority over this entire creation around us, and in abusing that power we also abuse creation and corrupt it. Back in Genesis, God tells Adam, "Cursed is the ground because of you" (Gen. 3:17). In other words, sin affects not only humankind, but all of creation. Today it's very clear that the earth around us suffers the curse of our bad stewardship. It is because of bad stewardship that we humans deal with one another worse than wolves deal with one another. It is because of bad stewardship that the Arctic glaciers retreat and the earth warms. It is because of bad stewardship that the air is polluted, the oceans are poisoned, and the land is poorly distributed.

Quite often, evils that we attribute to nature are partly our responsibility. For instance, because they have no place else to live, poor people frequently build their small huts in low lands that are subject to flooding. For several years, nothing happens. But then torrential rains flood the area, resulting in widespread death and great loss for those who have little they can afford to lose. In such cases, it is easy for us to blame the rain, forgetting that those who have suffered from the floods were living there because of human greed and sin.

In all of this, it commonly happens that, because we aren't willing to obey the directions of our Master, it becomes difficult for us to hear what the Master says. And then we say that God will not speak to us!

Such is the sad human condition. Like bad stewards, we deserve to be stripped of both our stewardship and the possession of what really belongs to the Master. But the justice of our eternal Master is far above the justice of earthly masters. The justice of our Master is such that it is the same as love. The justice of our Master is shown in surprising love. This will be the subject of our next chapter.

## For Reflection and Discussion

1. If we are made of the same dust as all animals, was St. Francis right when he spoke of "brother wolf"? Are we brothers and sisters of the wolf, the butterfly, and the ostrich? What characteristics do we share with brother wolf and the rest of the animals?

2. What distinguishes us from all of these "brothers and sisters"—that is, the rest of creation? In this chapter we have talked about our ability to transcend ourselves—to look at ourselves from the outside. Can you give any examples of this? (Have you ever had a dream in which it seemed like you were looking at yourself from the outside, as if you were watching yourself on a movie screen?) When you make plans for the future, are you in some measure looking at yourself from the outside?

3. How do you view the power and authority of humans over the rest of creation? What purposes and what limits do you think this power has?

4. In our relationship with nature, every day we learn more about it and how it functions, and therefore we acquire more power over it—or at least parts of it. Can this be part of God's purpose for our lives? Is it sometimes corrupted by sin? (Think, for instance, about the great advances that a deeper understanding of the structure of atoms has brought to nuclear medicine,

which saves many lives, and think at the same time of nuclear weapons, whose purpose is to destroy life.)

5. What do you think about the idea of taking the doctrine of the Trinity as an example for human relations? What values do you see in this? What dangers?

6. At the beginning of this chapter we dealt with a certain "absence" of God. How do you understand that absence? Have you ever experienced it? How does it connect to the manner in which you organize your life, manage your goods, and relate to other people and the rest of creation?

# FOUR

# Redemption: Jesus Christ and the New Creation

In Christianity there is no more important doctrine than that of redemption. What we affirm with this doctrine is that the God of creation, as a good parent, doesn't abandon it because of its disobedience. Like the father in the parable of the prodigal son, God awaits a return with open arms. Like the woman with the lost coin, God constantly seeks us. The doctrine of redemption affirms that, even despite our sin and our twisted ways, God still continues loving us and loving this entire creation.

It's important to stress this point because some Christians establish such a huge contrast between the first creation and the new creation that it would seem that God has abandoned a good part of the original creation. These thinkers and believers tend to speak of a material creation that God has little to do with, and a spiritual creation, particularly of souls, that is the only object of redemption and of God's love. This notion has no biblical foundation, but comes from a series of doctrines that were circulating during the first centuries of Christianity (and that still circulate) which affirm that only the spiritual world is important, and that the material world is either evil or irrelevant. The Bible speaks of a God who, upon creating the world, declared it to be good; and the Bible also affirms that this same God responds to our sin with restoring love.

## Seeing Christ in a Fallen Creation

The above is part of what we affirm when we proclaim the very core of the doctrine of redemption: the incarnation of God in Jesus Christ. Throughout the centuries the church has proclaimed that "in Christ God was reconciling the world to himself" (2 Cor. 5:19). In order to restore this fallen creation, God becomes part of it. That is love at its highest, and this is why we affirm that Jesus Christ is the highest and clearest revelation of God, of this God who above all is love.

On the other hand, Christians have long affirmed that this one whom we know in Jesus is the same Word of God that was in the beginning, through whom all things were made, and who is the light that illumines every human being. This is why we must insist on the continuity between the old creation and the new, between creation and redemption. They are both the work of the same God.

This affirmation gives positive value to the creation we see around us. Without forgetting that it is a fallen creation subjected to sin, we need to remember that it is still God's creation that we must love and respect, and over which we have been given a responsibility similar to that of ancient stewards.

But this is not all. This affirmation isn't limited to the physical creation that we see around us, but also includes human actions and thoughts. In those actions and thoughts there is certainly a good measure of evil, violence, and corruption. On the matter of actions, one need only mention domestic violence, unjust inequalities, and political corruption. As for thoughts, one can mention not only what we usually call "evil thoughts," but also all the errors in thinking and feeling circulating in today's world—idolatry, atheism, cynicism, and despair. Regarding such thoughts and feelings, we have to say something similar to what we said about physical creation: the same Word who in the beginning made all things still loves us and comes to us in the midst of such realities. This Word who is the light shining on every human who comes into the world is the same who illumines every good thought and every true knowledge.

For many early Christians this was of enormous importance. They lived in a world that considered itself wise, and had ample reason to boast about its wisdom. It was the world that had produced great philosophers such as Plato and Aristotle, the outstanding architects who built the Parthenon, and the Roman statesmen who were proud of their administrative order and the peace they believed it had brought to the Mediterranean basin. In the midst of such glories, Christians didn't seem to amount to much: they came from an obscure corner of the empire and had no great philosophers such as Plato. Given those circumstances, it would have been quite easy for believers simply to declare that all that was around them—the works of the philosophers, the Roman accomplishments in architecture and government, all the wisdom gathered through the centuries—was mere error and corruption, and that there was no good in the surrounding world. This is still a prevalent attitude in some Christian circles, where it would seem that all that doesn't come out of the church and doesn't express Christian doctrine is to be rejected, avoided, and even condemned. There were Christians in ancient times who adopted similar positions; but the majority clearly saw the need to affirm the presence and action of God even within this fallen world, and to see at least a vestige of God's truth even in those philosophers who didn't know God.

Basing their arguments partly on the very first few verses of the Gospel of John, early Christians affirmed that, since the Word who was in Jesus Christ is the same light that illumines every human being, every scintilla of light is due to the action and presence of the eternal Word of God. This makes it possible, even necessary, for us to claim whatever good there may be in the surrounding wisdom without setting aside the fundamental assertion that Jesus is the Truth made flesh.

A good example of this is found in St. Augustine's *Confessions*. As he tells the story of the process that eventually led him to conversion, he speaks of his attraction to Platonism—which at that time was considered the highest human knowledge. In this narrative of his spiritual pilgrimage, Augustine declares that in the books of the Platonists he found the affirmations that in the beginning was the Word, that the Word was with God, and that the Word was God.

But he also declares that in those writings he didn't find what the Gospel of John announces, that this Word came to his own—that is, was incarnate. In other words, Augustine understood that the great difference between Christian faith and any other philosophy, doctrine, or opinion, no matter how good it might be, is found precisely in verse 14 of the first chapter of John: "And the Word became flesh and lived among us, and we have seen his glory."

All this serves as a guide to understand how believers— who claim to be part of the new creation in Christ—can relate to all that has to do with the first creation. This includes the physical objects around us, the opinions and discoveries of others, the organization of society, and anything else we might imagine. On the basis of what John says, all of this shows the light of the eternal Word of God—of the Word that took flesh in Jesus Christ. For this reason, there is much in the surrounding world that we must affirm. But since this world is part of the old creation, there is also much in it that we must reject. And the difference, the touchstone letting us know which is which, is what we know of God's love and will through Scripture and through Jesus Christ.

At first this may seem very abstract, but it constantly has concrete relevance. If we forget that somehow the very fact that as humans we seek to organize ourselves in societies is the work of the Word of God, we will opt out of the social and political order as if it were demonic. If, on the other hand, we forget that the Word was incarnate in Christ, it becomes quite easy to fall into the opposite error: thinking that the existing social and political order, being the work of God, must be accepted just as it is. Between these two attitudes, Christian faith tells us that the world around us is still the object of the love of God, who made it; but that at the same time we must not look at it in such a way that we miss its injustices and corruption, or consider them unimportant.

## Understanding the Incarnate Christ

Throughout history, Christians have debated and written much about how it is possible for God to become human. In most cases, the problem has been that we imagine that we already know what being God means, and we define it in terms of a radical contrast with being human. Thus, for instance, we say that God is omnipotent, omniscient, omnipresent, and so on, and then ask ourselves how such a God can be uniquely present in a human being. As a result, the incarnation of the eternal God in a real human being at a particular time turns out to be a contradiction. But we can also begin at the other end, affirming that if we wish to know who and how God is, the best starting point is not speculation about the character of divinity, but rather this real human being, Jesus Christ the Lord. When we look at things in this way, the Incarnation is no longer an insoluble enigma, but rather an example and a calling. The Incarnation shows us what absolute communion between a human being and God is. This God who makes us after the divine image invites us to an ever-growing communion, following the example of Jesus himself. The true and deepest knowledge of God is reached not by means of intellectual speculation, but rather through what believers mean by the apparently simple phrase "following Jesus."

Even so, when thinking and speaking about Jesus, some will underscore his divinity, and others his humanity. Returning to the earlier example of doctrines as fences helping us to live freely and safely on a high plateau, we may say that the doctrine of the Incarnation does not tell us exactly how we are to understand the union of divinity and humanity in Jesus, but simply that we must avoid falling into the error of considering him a purely divine sort of ghost, as well as the opposite error of seeing him simply as an exceptional human being. And that we must also avoid the error of believing him to be partially divine and partially human.

Moving ahead, we may also say that the incarnation of God in Jesus Christ has a purpose. We have been and still are poor stewards, part of the fallen creation, but even so, God doesn't forsake us. God comes to seek us personally in Jesus Christ. This is the fundamental claim and experience that has supported the church through the centuries and still supports it. The incarnation of God in Jesus Christ is not above all a matter of speculation, but rather a reason for gratitude and wonder. It is here that we encounter God, in this human being of flesh and bone who lived, died, and was raised again.

When we read the New Testament looking for ways to understand who Jesus is and what he means for our faith and our life, we encounter first of all the picture of Jesus as Savior. This means that Jesus has come to rescue us from a condition of corruption and slavery to sin and death. We also find the image of Jesus as a teacher. This means that

Jesus has come to show us the way to the Father—a way of faith and obedience. We can also affirm that Jesus is Lord. This means that he is the sovereign master and ruler of all that we are and all that surrounds us. And we can go on listing other images that tell us something of Jesus and his work: Jesus is the Lamb of God who takes away the sins of the world (John 1:20); the new Adam and the beginning of the new creation (1 Cor. 15:45); the one in whom our lives are hidden, the first-begotten of all creation and also the first-begotten from among the dead, and the head of the church (Col. 1:15, 18; 3:3), the author of our salvation (Heb. 2:10); and many more.

The sheer variety of images shows us that it isn't possible to state in a few words or a single image all that Jesus means to us. All of these images together summarize and express a wide range of experiences of believers in their encounter with Jesus. Here again, as with the already mentioned plateau, we have complete freedom to stress any of those images, as long as we don't claim that thereby we've exhausted all that can be said about the bounteous work of Jesus for us.

One of the most common ways of speaking about Jesus is as a teacher. When using this image, we're emphasizing the point that Jesus came to provide us with lessons and examples that will lead us back to God. This is an important image, for there is no doubt that the New Testament presents Jesus as a teacher. Even on the cross he offers an important teaching about love and forgiveness. He is a teacher by means of his words, often expressed in parables, and also by means of actions such as his miracles and his meekness.

But to say that Jesus is only a great teacher is to leave aside much of the biblical witness.

Possibly the image that is most emphasized in our churches is that of Jesus as a payment in substitution for our sins. This image does have biblical foundations, and it's valuable because it acknowledges the seriousness of human sin. Sin is not an insignificant matter that one can easily undo or ignore; it's a condition that brings with it serious consequences. But this image by itself also entails certain risks. First among them is the danger that it may lead us to think of God as a severe moneylender who insists on being paid back down to the last penny. It also frequently leads some to think that God the Father is this severe one, while the Son is loving and forgiving. This contradicts all that the Bible tells us about who God is and about the relationship between the Son and the Father.

Finally, there is the image of Jesus as the victor over the powers of evil and the conqueror of death. This is the notion behind the words in Ephesians that Jesus "led captivity captive" (4:8). This image leads us to think of the life and work of Jesus as a drama of cosmic dimensions in which he faces the greatest powers of evil and overcomes them for our benefit.


### Understanding Jesus through the New Testament Story

As we read all that the New Testament says about the teachings of Jesus, we see that all of this is manifested in the story of his life. The story begins with the Annunciation and the birth of Jesus. We are told that the incarnation of God in a human being is a sign of the love of God, who comes to free us from our burden of sin. But it is also a lesson for us, as Paul makes clear in Philippians 2, where he invites his readers and us to have the same mind that was in Christ Jesus, who emptied himself and took the form of a servant. And it is also the first act of the cosmic drama in which God comes into creation in order to free it too from its bondage to sin. What we celebrate in Christmas is not just the birth of a child, but also a turning point in the victory of God over the powers of evil—a victory that begins in a humble manger.

The rest of the life of Jesus, leading to the events of Holy Week, is a series of teachings both by wise words and by wonderful works. But in these works Jesus also shows himself to be the powerful conqueror of evil.

We then come to the culmination of the entire work of Jesus, which is his death and resurrection. Quite correctly, Christianity has centered its attention on the cross. The cross is not only a tragedy and an injustice, but is also the greatest proof of God's love for us. The God who comes to be one of us in the Incarnation suffers on the cross the most wretched death that humans may suffer: the just for the unjust. This is what we mean by "atonement." In everyday language we use similar expressions when we say, for instance, that a convict in jail is making atonement for his crimes or is paying for them. Just as crime has consequences for those who commit it, so sin has its price. As Paul says, "the wages of sin is death." But this loving God of ours, rather than demanding our death, offers to suffer on the cross in our stead. This is why Paul not only says that the wages of sin is death, but also says that "the free gift of God is eternal life in Christ Jesus our Lord" (Rom. 6:23). Therefore, we see Jesus dying for our sin on the cross. But on that same cross, Jesus, while being a sacrificial victim in our place, continues being a teacher—one who provides us with an exemplary teaching by praying for those who crucify him. And we can also see in the cross a second act in the cosmic drama, so that the one who at the Incarnation came to be one of us will, in subjecting himself to death, now enter the very abode of the powers of evil in order to conquer death and evil.

That victory comes at the Resurrection, which is not just a sign or proof that the one who gave himself up on the cross was divine, but is also the great victory or third act of the cosmic drama. The God who became incarnate on that first Christmas and who suffered on that sorrowful Good Friday—that God on the third day rose again from among the dead, thus conquering death itself and all the powers of evil. It is interesting to note that in the most ancient art that we have depicting the resurrection of Jesus, we see him breaking down the gates of hell and freeing the captives held there. This is why some ancient Christian writers celebrate and affirm that on that Easter morning Jesus "killed death."

We then come to the Ascension, an event that frequently passes unnoticed. The Ascension is the victory of the Crucified One, who is now sitting at the right hand of the Father. But, since this one who is seated at the Father's right hand is also a human being, the Ascension is the first fruits of our own victory.

Finally, all of this points to the glorious day of the final consummation, when "at the name of Jesus every knee should bend, in heaven and on earth and under the earth" (Phil. 2:10).

This can be expressed in other words: we can affirm, for instance, that Jesus comes down to us so that we may rise to the presence of the heavenly throne, and that he becomes a victim in our stead so that in his victory we may also be victorious over all the powers that oppress us, including sin and death.

This is also what the New Testament means when speaking of Jesus as the new Adam. The Word of God, who was in the beginning of creation and through whom all things were made, has now entered his own creation in order to lead it to its fulfillment. As Paul says, while the first Adam was given life, this second Adam gives life (1 Cor. 15:45). Just as the old Adam is head of all the fallen human race, the new Adam is head of a new and restored humankind (a subject to which we will return when speaking of the church as the body of Christ).

### Understanding Justification and Predestination

At this point it is wise to deal with the theme of justification. As is commonly known, one of the main emphases of the Protestant Reformation was "justification by faith." A well-known story involves Martin Luther's experience of profound angst because he couldn't understand how he, a sinner, could present himself before a God who is pure, just, and holy. In the midst of that angst, when reading in the letter to the Romans that "the just shall live by faith" (Rom.

1:17), Luther came to the conclusion that justification is not a human task, but the work of God which we may appropriate and in which we may trust through faith. Faith doesn't make us just. Rather, faith enables us to hear the unexpected verdict of the grace of God, declaring us free from sin. Again, justification is not something that we do, but something that God does for us.

This doesn't mean that good works aren't necessary. But it does mean that such works don't justify us or make us more worthy in God's eyes. Good works are necessary not because they save us, but simply because they are the necessary result of true faith. There's no such thing as a good faith that produces no good works. But to imagine that our good works gain salvation for us is to deny the enormity of our sin and its contrast with God's holiness. This is what we mean by "justification by faith." Such faith is not simply a more subtle sort of work, so that our faith saves us. It is God who saves us, and faith leads us to see and accept that salvation and to rest on its promise.

Finally, still on the subject of how we attain salvation—or perhaps it would be better to say how salvation comes to us—we must at least mention the much-debated issue of predestination and free will. At this point we have to set aside the caricatures that are often built around these two positions. On the one hand, there is an enormous difference between predestination and determinism. The latter means that everything is already predetermined—that if I'm writing these lines, it's because God determined that it would be so before the foundation of the world; and that if you read them, you will be doing so for the same reason. The theological affirmation of predestination has nothing to do with such determinism. Predestination is simply an affirmation that if we believe, this is due primarily to the work of God, not to our own decision as good people. On the other hand, free will doesn't mean, as we often imagine, that we have such freedom that someday, without divine help or intervention, we can simply decide that we're going to believe in God. Rather, it means that God doesn't force us to believe, that our accepting by faith the justification that God offers us is an expression of our own free will.

Each of these two affirmations has its place and its purpose. The doctrine of predestination makes it impossible for us to boast of our own faith, or to think that we are more worthy than those who don't believe. Salvation is above all a gift from God. The doctrine of free will prevents those who don't wish to accept God's offer of justification from blaming God for it, when in fact it is their own will that stands in the way. Both doctrines are necessary, because those who believe have no right to claim any merit, and those who don't believe have no excuse.

The reason why this matter has led to endless debate and to bitter divisions in the church is that we've forgotten what was said at the very beginning of this book about doctrines as fences that keep us away from dangerous cliffs. The doctrine of predestination warns us about the danger of spiritual pride that boasts of its own faith. The doctrine of free will warns us against the other extreme, because if we go too far in the direction of predestination, we run the risk of blaming God for our bad decisions. The error into which we have repeatedly fallen, on both sides, is to think that these doctrines, rather than being warnings against serious mistakes, are absolute and literal descriptions of reality—as if it were possible for the human mind to understand the secret designs of God.

### For Reflection and Discussion

1. Christians affirm that Jesus is both divine and human. What would be the consequences of claiming that Jesus is purely divine? What would be the consequences of claiming that he's purely human?

2. If we affirm that Jesus is truly God and truly human, what does this tell us about God? What does it tell us about what it means to be truly human?

3. In this chapter I mention various ways of speaking about Jesus and what he does for us. Which of these speaks most clearly to your experience? Why?

4. What positive value do you see in the doctrine of predestination? What positive value do you see in the doctrine of free will? What would happen if we thought only in terms of predestination, as if there were no such thing as freedom of the human will? What would happen if we thought only in terms of free will, as if our salvation didn't depend on God's will?

# FIVE

# The Spirit of Holiness

In the last chapter we saw that God justifies us in Jesus Christ. Justification means that God declares us just, not on the basis of our own justice, but rather on the justice of Christ. Still, this doesn't imply that God is content with declaring us just and leaving us the same as we were, wallowing in sin and corrupted by it. Although we often speak of salvation as if it were only a promise of eternal life in the presence of God, in truth it is that and much more; it is also the process by which the God who declares us just by divine grace continues to work in our lives in such a way that they will more clearly reflect the purposes of God. This is what we call sanctification. Thus, salvation includes not only justification, but also sanctification. To make things very clear: we must insist that God doesn't justify us because we are holy, but rather that God calls us to holiness because we have been justified.

Put another way, this means that God doesn't forgive us by virtue of our own holiness. What actually happens is that the God who loves and justifies us even while we are sinners still loves us and continues working in us so that each day we will be more as we ought to be.

One way of understanding this may be to think of the connection and difference between a cure and health. Certainly, a person who is sick needs a cure. But such a cure is not the same as health. A cure is an answer and a remedy to a bad condition. Once healed, one has to go through a process of restoration in order to be truly healthy. Just as a cure remains incomplete without health, so justification remains incomplete without sanctification.

Throughout the ages, several Christian writers have expressed this reality and its relationship with the Holy Spirit by affirming that without the Holy Spirit there is no salvation. Firstly, we cannot be saved without the Holy Spirit because in order to confess Jesus Christ as Lord, we must do so by the Spirit. This is why Paul declares that "no one can say 'Jesus is Lord' except by the Holy Spirit" (1 Cor. 12:3). Naturally, by this Paul means not simply being able to pronounce the words, but rather having Jesus Christ as Lord. Secondly, we cannot be saved without the Holy Spirit because salvation is not limited to justification, but also includes sanctification, which is the specific work of the Holy Spirit. Thus, the Spirit is active at the very beginning of faith, leading us to the risen Christ and making us part of his body. And then the same Spirit guides us into sanctification as members of the body of Christ.

## Who Is the Holy Spirit?

Just as justification is not our work, but rather the work of
Jesus Christ, so also sanctification is not our work, but rather
the work of the Holy Spirit. Sadly, the doctrine of the Holy
Spirit has not always received the attention it is due. As a
result, when speaking of the Holy Spirit we quite often focus
on matters that, while important, are secondary. This leads
us to two considerations.

In the first place, it is important to stress that the Holy
Spirit is God. The Spirit is just as divine as the Father or the
Son. Like the Son, the Spirit exists from all eternity. God is
eternally Father, Son, and Holy Spirit. While it is true that
in the church we experience the promises of the Holy Spirit,
it is also true that from the very beginning of creation the
Spirit of God was moving over the face of the waters (Gen.
1:2). And it is equally true that the incarnation of God in
Jesus Christ takes place by the work of the Holy Spirit (Luke
1:35). To ignore the Holy Spirit is to ignore God. To listen to
and obey the Holy Spirit is to listen to and obey God.

The second important point has to do with the work of
the Holy Spirit among us. As already stated, the Bible tells us
that it's impossible truly to confess Jesus Christ without being
led to it by the Holy Spirit. In other words, it's not a matter
of first believing in Jesus and then having the Spirit guide us.
The very fact that we believe in Jesus is already a manifestation of the presence of the Holy Spirit. Since the Holy Spirit is
God, wherever we see God acting, the Holy Spirit is present.

Part of the reason why much traditional theology has
paid insufficient attention to the Holy Spirit may be lack of

72

interest. But a more important reason lies in the difficulty of speaking of one who, like the wind, flows in unexpected ways (John 3:8). The freedom of the Spirit reminds us of the absolute sovereignty of God, whom we cannot box in by our definitions and expectations. It is precisely when speaking and thinking of the Holy Spirit that we see more clearly the impossibility of corralling God.

We can see this clearly in Scripture. In Acts 8 we're told that believers in Samaria received the Holy Spirit when the apostles laid their hands on them. This might lead us to affirm that in order to receive the Holy Spirit, one must first believe and then receive the Spirit through the imposition of hands. But in Acts 10, Cornelius and those in his household receive the Spirit before they have been baptized— actually, Peter decides to baptize them because they show that they have received the Spirit. In most instances in the Bible, the Spirit moves believers to proclaim their faith, but in Acts 16:6 we find the surprising assertion that Paul and his companions were "forbidden by the Holy Spirit to speak the word in Asia." Sometimes the Holy Spirit comes to an individual believer, but in Acts 13:2 the Spirit, rather than speaking directly to Paul and Barnabas, tells the believers, "Set apart for me Barnabas and Saul for the work to which I have called them." All of this clearly shows that when we speak about the work of the Holy Spirit, we must do so with a care similar to that of Moses before the burning bush, for we are standing on holy ground.

## Understanding the Gifts of the Spirit

With this background, we can focus on the specific work of the Spirit in sanctifying believers and the church. The Holy Spirit acts in individual Christians for our sanctification. And the same Spirit acts in the church for its sanctification. This means that, while we celebrate what are often called the "extraordinary gifts" of the Spirit—gifts such as speaking in tongues and healing—the purpose of all of these gifts is sanctification. We can see this clearly in Paul's first epistle to the Corinthians, in whose chapter 12 Paul speaks of the great variety of gifts of the Holy Spirit and how each of them has a place in building up the body of Christ. Here Paul uses the image of the church as a body in which each member has a particular function according to the gifts each has received. None of the members may boast of particular gifts, as if the others weren't important. All of these gifts—prophecy, teaching, performing miracles, healing, speaking in tongues, and many more—are the work of the Holy Spirit for the upbuilding of the body. Therefore, all these gifts deserve equal respect and gratitude. That is why, if someone believes or claims that by having a particular gift and not another he is more important than the rest, it is like saying to the hand of the body, "I don't need you." All the gifts of the Spirit are equally important to the body of Christ, and therefore those who receive them have to work harmoniously among themselves.

What must be stressed in all of this—and what is often forgotten—is that the gifts of the Spirit are not primarily for our individual benefit, but are rather gifts for the church community, which is the body of Christ. This is why at the end of chapter 12, after speaking of the gifts of the Spirit and encouraging his readers to seek them, Paul says, "I will show you a still more excellent way." That more excellent way is love, as may be seen in the very next verses: "If I speak in the tongues of mortals and of angels, but do not have love, I am a noisy gong or a clanging cymbal. And if I have prophetic powers, and understand all mysteries and all knowledge, and if I have all faith, so as to remove mountains, but do not have love, I am nothing" (1 Cor. 13:1–2).

Throughout the history of the church, when discussing the gifts of the Holy Spirit, many believers have fallen into one of two errors. On the one hand, sometimes we act as if the order of the church—what we humans understand by order—is more important than the freedom of the Spirit. In that case, if someone speaks in strange tongues or refers to a miracle, he or she is silenced or excluded, as if the head were able to tell the feet, "I don't need you." On the other hand, sometimes the gifts of the Holy Spirit are understood in an exceedingly individualistic fashion, as if they were gifts for the benefit of a particular believer, and not for the church as a whole. In such cases, sometimes Christians even fall into a spirit of competition, some claiming to have better gifts than others. It is to this that Paul refers in chapter 14 of his first epistle to the Corinthians, where he insists that when it comes to the gifts of the Spirit, they should "strive to excel in them *for building up the church*" (1 Cor. 14:12; my emphasis).

Perhaps once again we may be helped by the image of doctrines as fences preventing our falling into possible errors. The entire church lives on this high plateau, on which we move freely by the grace of God. At one edge of the plateau there is the dangerous cliff of wishing to limit and control the action of the Holy Spirit in the life of the church. In order to avoid that error, we must remember what Jesus himself said about the Spirit, who is like the wind, blowing where it wills (John 3:8). But at the other edge of the plateau there is the opposite error into which we may fall, which is to forget that the gifts of the Spirit are given to us primarily for the upbuilding of the church, and not for our own personal joy or individual boasting. When we fall into the first error, the church loses its vitality, for we are no longer ready to have God surprise us or interrupt the order and expectations that we have created. When we fall into the second error, the church loses its unity, with each of us seeking after particular individual gifts, and even competing among ourselves. Between these two errors is the clear fact that the Spirit gives us whatever gifts the Spirit wishes, and when the Spirit wishes.

## The Holy Spirit and Sanctification

It is to the upbuilding of the church that we refer when we speak of sanctification, both of individuals and of the church as a whole. Even though in the process of sanctification the Holy Spirit acts with sovereign freedom, we must also remember that this Spirit is the same who inspired Scripture and still speaks to us in it, and that therefore the Bible is the best guide we have in the process of sanctification. If we forget that justification is the work of God, not us, the

biblical text frequently takes us back to the heavy burden of
the law that we cannot fulfill. This is what Paul means when
he says that "no human being will be justified in [God's]
sight by deeds prescribed by the law" (Rom. 3:20). As law, the
Bible shows us how far we are from what we ought to be.
Sadly, too often we stay there, and then become embittered
Christians who seem to think that our task is to impose the
same burden on others. At that point Christianity becomes
a matter of "Don't do this" and "Don't do that," under threat
of eternal fire.

But when we truly understand that God justifies us out
of loving divine grace, and not because of our holiness or
our obedience to the law, this law that previously seemed
bitter turns sweet, for now the commandment becomes a
promise.

We may take the very first of the Ten Commandments as
an example: "You shall have no other gods before me" (Exod.
20:3). Taking this commandment seriously, as we should,
may well become a heavy burden. The truth is that we all
have alien gods before God. For some of us, it's money; for
others, prestige; for others, their own ambition; for others,
success; for others, their family; and so on. Even though we
don't call such things gods, in actual practice they are. They
rule our lives just as the ancient pagan gods ruled the lives
of their followers, and we offer sacrifices before their al-
tars just as the ancients offered sacrifices to their own gods.
Thus, having no other gods before God turns out to be an
unreachable goal, and the commandment itself condemns
us. But when we understand that we are justified by the
grace of God, and that the Holy Spirit is acting in us for our

sanctification, we can also read the same commandment as a promise: "You will have no other gods. . . ." In other words, the day will come when we truly will have no other gods before us. This God promises us, not because of who we are or because of what we do, but because of what the Holy Spirit is doing within us.

All of this leads us to an important fact that we often forget: our holiness is not based on our being saintly, pure, or less sinful than others, but is rooted in our being joined to a most holy head: Christ himself. This is why we ought not to be surprised that Paul refers to the Corinthians as "saints," and then speaks of all sorts of sin and dissension among them. These Corinthians are saints not because they're good, but because the Holy Spirit moves among them and makes them part of the body of Christ. Clearly, it is expected that such saints will live following the will of God, but this is not what makes them saints. Being a saint is not being "holier than thou." The "holier than thou" understanding of holiness inverts the order of things, as if it were good works that make us holy, when in fact it is the holiness that we receive by the power of the Holy Spirit that leads us to seek to live according to the will of God and therefore to do good works.

Sometimes, precisely because we forget this difference between true holiness and the "holier than thou" attitude, we draw a picture of a holy person as an austere and embittered one whose attention is often devoted to pointing out the sin of others. True holiness is joyful, for it is a life based on the promises of God, and it is therefore a life of love such as is described in 1 Corinthians 13.

78

## How the Holy Spirit Works

As a further way to understand the manner in which the Holy Spirit works, it may be helpful to consider again what took place on that Pentecost day after the Ascension, as told in Acts 2. The first thing we note in this passage is that, unlike what we often think and see in classical paintings about Pentecost, the Spirit did not come only over the apostles and leaders. "They were *all* together in one place. . . . *All of them* were filled with the Holy Spirit." The gift of the Spirit is not limited to the leaders of the church or to a few particular individuals, but may well come to every believer. Then, we are also told that this gift comes within the context of unity: "they were all *together* in one place" (2:1–4; my emphasis). Too often we think that because we have received a special gift from the Spirit, this sets us apart from others; sometimes we even come to the point of imagining that if we receive such a gift, it is because we are holier than others. But that is not the case. It is not our holiness that brings the Spirit, but rather the Spirit who brings holiness. The plateau image again becomes useful here. If at one edge we have the cliff of an order and a hierarchy that impede the mission of the church by not allowing believers to be led by the Holy Spirit, at the other extreme we have the cliff of employing a supposed manifestation of the Holy Spirit as a reason to consider ourselves superior to others and so withdraw from them.

The inclusivity of the gift of the Spirit that we can see in that Pentecost account in the repeated use of the word "all" is also at the very heart of the words that Peter uses to explain what's taking place. When some mock the group by claiming that they're drunk, Peter tells them that what they're seeing is the fulfillment of the prophecy of Joel: "Your sons and your daughters shall prophesy, and your young men shall see visions, and your old men shall dream dreams" (Acts 2:17). In other words, the outpouring of the Spirit produces an inclusivity and equality among men and women, young and old. The presence of the Holy Spirit doesn't create divisions or place some above others, but does exactly the opposite.

It is also important to note that this passage also stresses cultural inclusivity. If the purpose of the outpouring of the Holy Spirit was that all would be able to hear the gospel, this could have been achieved in one of two ways. One possibility would have been to make all understand the Aramaic that the apostles and most of the others spoke. Another would have been to have each understand in their own tongue. The first alternative would have given the language and culture of the first disciples a particular and permanent dominance. The second one, which is what actually takes place, is an affirmation of the possibility and the need to have the gospel proclaimed and be incarnate equally in every language and culture.

Finally, a word on "inspiration." This is a word often employed in relation to the work of the Holy Spirit. It is a very adequate term, particularly if we remember that the verb "to inspire," which in common usage refers to having an influence on a person or a movement, is related to words for the breathing process. We breathe in—inspire—to fill our lungs with air. Christian life without the Holy Spirit is as impossible as human life without oxygen. If it was the Holy Spirit who inspired the apostles and prophets in their writing, it is that very Spirit who today inspires us in our reading. The Bible is the Word of God because the same Spirit who inspired its writing now inspires its reading.

On this score, we must note that in the Gospels the devil himself employs the Bible in order to tempt Jesus. It is possible to use the Bible in order to attack others or to justify our own actions, attributes, and preferences. But when the Bible is used without that love which is the highest gift of the Spirit, it is being used in a twisted fashion, as the devil employed it in tempting Jesus. The Bible is the Word of God for us when we read it under the inspiration of the same Spirit who inspired its writers. This is a Spirit of love. As Paul says, without love we are nothing.

## For Reflection and Discussion

1. Read John 2:8. What is the similarity between the wind and the Holy Spirit? Does the word "inspire" help us understand that similarity? Is it true that, just as we cannot live without inspiring oxygen, the church cannot live without the inspiration of the Holy Spirit?

2. Do you believe that we have the Holy Spirit because we are holy, or rather that we are holy because we have the Holy Spirit? What concrete difference does this make in our life as believers and in the life of the church as a body?

3. We say that the Bible is the Word of God because it was inspired by the Holy Spirit. If we try to read it without

the help of that same Spirit, is it still the Word of God
for us?

4. If we read the Bible claiming and hoping that we are
doing so inspired by the Holy Spirit, does the church
have a role in our interpretation of Scripture? What
connection exists between that role and the doctrines
the church sets up as "fences at the edges of the
plateau"?

# SIX

# The Church: A Community of the Holy Spirit

As we have seen, the main purpose of the gifts of the Spirit is the upbuilding of the body of Christ. Therefore, as soon as we begin thinking about the Holy Spirit, we also have to take the church into consideration. To be a believer in Christ is by definition also to be part of his body. He is the head, and those of us who believe in him are members of the body. Just as the members of our bodies live only because they share in the entire life of the body, so we who call ourselves Christians can be such only through our participation in his body.

This focus requires that we clarify what we mean by "church." In its widest and also most exact meaning, the church is the totality of all those who believe in Jesus Christ and are grafted into him in a way similar to that in which members form part of the body, or as a branch is grafted into the vine (John 15:5). It is in this sense that we often speak of the "invisible church." There is a positive use for this term, for the church includes countless people, both in the past and in the present, whom we have never seen gathered and who are not part of a single organization. But, on the other hand, the church must always be visible. The church is not a purely spiritual reality with no tangible manifestations in history and in present life. On the contrary, the church always exists concretely, and is present wherever there is a community of believers.

## What Is the Church?

What does all of this mean? First, it means that the church of Jesus Christ is not limited to a particular organization. We cannot say that those who don't belong to our ecclesial organization are therefore not part of the church. As Paul clearly says in Corinthians, the eye cannot claim that it does not need the hand, nor can the head say that it does not need the feet.

Second, the preceding also means that being a believer in Christ is also being a member of his body, and that therefore it is impossible to be a true believer without being part of this vast community of the faithful that extends over centuries and continents. And, since this community exists always in concrete communities, an essential part of Christian life is belonging to and participating in a church community.

Thirdly, the distinction between visible churches and the invisible church means that the mere fact of belonging to the visible church is no guarantee that we are members of the invisible church. As we well know, in the visible church there are, amid much wheat, also tares. However, as the parable teaches us, it is not our task to determine who is wheat and who is not, who belongs to the invisible church and who does not.

All of this leads us to the words of our brother Cyprian, who was bishop of Carthage in North Africa almost eighteen centuries ago. According to him, "one cannot have God as Father who does not have the church as mother." Naturally, these few words have been much debated and interpreted in a variety of ways. Quite often they have been misunderstood, in the sense that anyone who doesn't belong to a particular church organization cannot be a true believer in Jesus Christ. In other words, if the church of Christ were only and exclusively one of the visible churches, this would mean that the leaders of that church would be like guardians at the gate into the reign of God. But if the invisible church, which includes all those who are members of Christ's body, is manifested in a multitude of visible churches, Cyprian's saying doesn't mean that any one of these churches is the custodian of the reign of God. What it does mean is that all who declare themselves to be believers in Christ, and therefore children of the Father, must be connected with other members of the same body. The normal expression of that connection is one of the many visible churches that we see everywhere. It is by participating in those communities that we are also participants in the body of Christ, and therefore in his life.

The church is—or ought to be—the place where we practice and announce a love that points to the reign of God and prepares us for it. This is one of the reasons why diversity within the church is so important. In society at large, we tend to create communities among people we like. The same happens in the church. But this isn't enough. If we stop at that point, the church simply becomes one of those many communities, and will simply resemble a social club with religious overtones. The church is called to be a place where we learn and practice a love that goes beyond our particular tastes and shared interests. The church is called to be an announcement and a foretaste of the reign of God. This is precisely the reason why dissension within the church is so harmful: it is an attempt against the very nature of the church. And this is also the reason why it is important for our present community not to be limited to a group of people who are all alike. In order to be a true school preparing us for the reign, the church must manifest a diversity similar to that which we expect in the reign.

In the face of this, someone might object by saying that it's possible to become a Christian by simply reading the Bible, and that this shows that the church isn't necessary. But the very fact that somehow that Bible came into that person's hands shows that even this apparently isolated person is in fact part of the community of faith. It may be a community that one doesn't know, but without it the Bible would never have reached that person's hands. Furthermore, in the Bible itself the community witnesses to its faith, and therefore that isolated believer becomes part of a community that includes those first disciples (people such as Peter, John, Mary, Paul, and Priscilla), all the disciples throughout the ages, and those who are now living. Furthermore, if that solitary person reads the Bible and understands it, this in itself will involve a call to seek or to form a community of believers in which one can live that foretaste of the reign of God.

Even so, today we frequently encounter people who tell us that it's possible for them to be Christians without the church. This is partly due to the poor witness of many believers whose bitter animosity, intellectual narrowness, and attitudes of moralizing judgment lead those who see them to seek a different way of being Christian. It is also due to the desire on the part of many to be Christians after their own fashion, without having anyone else interfere in their lives. But the fact is that, while every human community is imperfect, we have been made for life in community, and we deceive ourselves if we think we really can live outside of any such body. If the imperfections of our countries and our cultures don't keep us from loving our native lands and rejoicing in our culture, we cannot claim imperfections within the church as an excuse not to be part of it. To this will be added the calling of the church to be better than any of those communities. The church is called to lead a life such that it is both an announcement and a foretaste of the reign of God.

## How Is the Church Holy?

There is no doubt that no matter how much we try to avoid them, in the church there will be not only those disagreements which are necessary and useful in reaching wise decisions, but also less commendable reasons for dissension—gossip, resentment, politicking. While we seek to avoid such things, we must constantly confess that we are not free from them. That confession itself is part of the mission of the church. The church doesn't exist to show the world how pure it is, but rather to show the world how much God loves us despite our impurity. When the church pretends to be purer than the rest of humanity, and on that basis rejects the "sinners," it is missing a chance to show the richness of God's grace. Thus, while part of the mission of the church is to be a foretaste of the future that God has promised, part of its mission is also the knowledge that we don't expect that future by virtue of our own purity, but rather by virtue of the grace of a God who forgives us and who offers the same forgiveness to the rest of humankind.

All of this must be joined to what we discussed in the previous chapter regarding the gifts of the Holy Spirit and their connection with the church. Once again, these gifts are given for the upbuilding of the body of Christ. This is the reason why, in many of the ancient creeds of the church, the two are joined together: "I believe in the Holy Spirit, the holy catholic church. . . ." (I will say more on the word "catholic" later on.)

Believing in the church doesn't mean believing whatever the leaders of the church tell us. Rather, it means that those of us who believe do so "in" the church, within it, participating in it, resting on it. And we can do this because we also believe and rest "in" the Holy Spirit, who is the link joining all the members of this body that is the church to Jesus Christ, its head, as well as to one another.

At this point we need to clarify what we mean by the word "holy" as applied to the church. If our own holiness is the work of the Holy Spirit, the same is true for the holiness of the church. And, just as our holiness is not in our purity, but rather in the presence in us of the Holy Spirit and in our union with Christ, who is holy, so does the holiness of the church not depend on its purity. The church is holy not because its members are pure, but rather because the Holy Spirit joins it to its holy head, Jesus Christ, and because the Spirit is holy.

This is fundamentally important, for if we believe that our holiness consists in our purity, and that the holiness of the church also depends on its purity, we shall constantly be seeking a purer church. The practical result, as we see daily, is that a body that considers itself purer than the rest withdraws in order to create a holier church. Shortly thereafter, another group will appear in that church and that will consider itself pure and will once again break away in order to create an even purer church. Tragically, such supposed holiness contradicts and impedes the work of the Holy Spirit, which is a work of unity and love.

This doesn't mean that sin within the church is a matter of little importance. On the contrary, precisely because the church is holy by reason of the presence of the Holy One in it, every stain of sin in the church is a profanation of God's holiness. This is true of each of us individually as well as of the church as a whole. As believers, we know that we are sinners, and we even suspect that there are in our lives grave sins that are hidden even to ourselves. If we forget the grace of God, this may lead us to a sense of guilt and unspeakable anguish that grows until we come to hate ourselves. Such, for instance, was the experience of Martin Luther when he was seeking all possible means to get rid of his sin and was unable to do so, with the result that he was constantly torn. This anguish can be resolved only by God's grace, when we discover that God loves us, justifies us, and even calls us "holy," not by virtue of our own purity, but of divine grace. All of this is also true of the church: God loves it, uses it, and calls it "holy," not because it is pure in itself, but because God is loving. Therefore, the church is not holy because of its purity, just as we are not holy because we are pure; rather, the church is holy by virtue of the love and grace by which the only Holy One sustains it.

All of this means that sin, both in our individual lives and in the community of the church, is much more serious than we would otherwise imagine. Just as sin in believers profanes God's holiness, so does sin in the church. Although God does forgive sin, both in individuals and in the church, this doesn't mean that sins are not a grave matter. On the contrary, the very fact that God calls us and the church "holy" makes our sin more damnable. And just as the answer of individual believers to our sin must be confession and an appeal to God's mercy, so does the answer of the church to its own sin have to be confession and appeal to the same mercy. This is why throughout the centuries in the worship of the church there have been moments and times in which we confess our sin and call on God's grace.

In all this we must remember that the work of the Holy Spirit is not only a process of joining us to the body of Christ and therefore making us participants in his holiness, but also a process of sanctification, which is the necessary result of our justification. While it is true that God declares us holy because by virtue of the Holy Spirit we are joined to the holy head of the church, it is also true that the Holy Spirit has been given for our sanctification. Anyone who refuses to follow this process of sanctification that is part of salvation is resisting the Holy Spirit. This happens, for instance, when someone says, "I know that I should forgive him, but I can't. That's just who I am." Perhaps that truly is who I am; but the work of the Holy Spirit is to make me what I am not but should be. Therefore, simply to excuse our sin by saying that this is who we are is to reject the work of the Holy Spirit in ourselves.

## What Is a "catholic" Church?

Moving on to a different subject, most ancient creeds—including those used today, such as the Apostles' Creed and the Nicene Creed—speak of the church as "catholic." This is a source of some confusion, for today there is a particular church that is commonly known as the Catholic Church. For this reason, many Protestant churches, instead of affirming belief in the "catholic" church, refer to it as the "universal" church or simply the "Christian" church.

The word "universal" means that the church in which we believe is present throughout the world and throughout the ages. This is important, because the church to which we belong, the true church of Jesus Christ, is not only a group that gathers in a particular place, but all those who gather all over the world. Nor is it limited to the believers of our time, but includes the many others who have gone before us and whose heirs we are. When we say we believe in the church, we're declaring that we believe, yes, in this church in which we congregate periodically and which supports us directly in our faith; but we're also declaring that we believe that this church with which we gather is part of the same body of Christ to which belong all Christians who live today in Namibia, China, and Germany, as well as those who lived in centuries past in Italy, Manchuria, and Congo.

However, in affirming that we believe in the "universal" church, and thus ignoring or abandoning the word "catholic," we risk losing something of great importance, for this latter word has some dimensions and connotations that don't come up in the same way when we speak of something as "universal." Etymologically, the word "catholic" is derived from two Greek roots. The first of these two roots means "according to." It is the same word that appears in the titles of the Gospels that we translate as "the Gospel according to . . ." (Matthew, Mark, Luke, and John). There is a single gospel of Jesus Christ, and it comes to us through four witnesses. The expression "according to" points to a diversity of perspectives and ways of understanding the one and only gospel. The second root of the word "catholic" means "the whole" or "all." It is the same root that we find, for instance, in the word "hologram," which refers to an image that includes a holistic view in three dimensions.

Thus, when in the ancient Christian church people spoke of something being "catholic," this involved a diversity of perspectives which together give the picture a depth similar to that of a hologram. This is why, when speaking of the Four Gospels, they spoke of them as the "catholic witness" to the gospel of Jesus Christ. Together, these Four Gospels, in their very diversity, witness to a single reality, but each from its own perspective. Likewise, in affirming faith in the "catholic" church, ancient Christians were affirming their faith and participation in the church with different emphases and perspectives, but in which all shared the same faith and witnessed to it. In this sense, any claim on the part of any particular church or Christian community to be the only true church, therefore rejecting others, opposes the catholicity that the early church experienced and that we affirm in the creeds. The opposite of being "catholic" is being sectarian, and therefore any Christian community, large or small, which insists that it alone is the church of Jesus Christ is in truth a sect. At this point it may be helpful to see the etymological relationship between the word "sect" and the word "section." A sect is any group that takes a part or a section as if it were the whole. That is, a sect is any church that claims to be the whole church and rejects the rest. Over against such sectarian tendencies, which lead us to think that our way of understanding things, our experience of faith, and our cultural or particular perspectives are normative, John, the writer of Revelation, tells us of "a great multitude that no one could count, from every nation, from all tribes and peoples and languages" (Rev. 7:9).

Concretely, this is shown in the diversity of expressions of faith, ways of worshiping, and systems of government that exist within the church of Jesus Christ. In the following chapter we will deal more fully with worship, but we all know that in the church today there is a multitude of ways of worship. Great variety also exists in the organization and government within churches. Some have bishops, and others not. Some churches have a congregational form of government—that is, a polity in which each congregation governs itself independently from the rest. In many others, while congregations have some authority over their own lives, means are found to create wider circles of responsibility. Although sometimes some insist that their form of government is the only one that is acceptable, in fact each of these various forms can find support in the New Testament, and they all also reflect various cultural origins. These differences, which may well lead to confusion, are actually witnesses to the variety of perspectives and experiences that are fundamental elements in the catholicity of the church. Each of these forms of government has something to contribute to the totality of the church.

## Understanding the Church's Mission

Having discussed these things, we must remember not to center our attention on the church itself as a community, and much less on the church as an organization. The most important element in the life of the church is not its organization or its doctrines. What is most important in the life of the church is its mission. It is not a matter of first becoming a church and then discovering a mission, but the opposite. Paleontologists tell us that when aquatic animals began to emerge from the water in order to live on land, they evolved in such a way that they developed legs. They did not first have legs and then set out to find ways to use them. Rather, the very fact of making their way beyond the water led to the development of the necessary instruments. Something similar happens with the church. What gives shape to the church is its mission. For this reason many say that where there is no mission, there is no church. A church centered on itself, no matter how much faith its members have, is not a faithful church.

Sometimes we limit the mission of the church to that which it does when it looks outward, calling sinners, serving the needy, preaching in distant lands. But the inner life of the church is also part of its mission. It is in the inner life that we learn to practice a love that goes beyond the social, economic, cultural, and political links that govern social relations. That inner life of the church immediately becomes an outward witness. As Jesus himself said, "By this everyone will know that you are my disciples, if you love one another" (John 13:35). And somewhat later, in the midst of persecutions late in the second century and early in the third, Tertullian tells us that pagans said about Christians, "See how they love one another."

The heart of the mission of the church is giving witness to the purpose of God for all of creation. Within this fallen creation, within this self-seeking humanity, and within this corrupt society, the first purpose of the church is to show this creation, this humankind, and this society that there is a different order possible, and that such an order is God's ultimate design. The foundation of the mission of the church is in giving witness within the present order, which in truth is a sort of disorder, to a different order: within the disorder of violence, to an order of peace; within the disorder of abuse

95

and injustice, to an order of service and justice; within the disorder in a society in which all seek their own good, to an order of love in which all seek what is good for the neighbor.

All of this means that the very core of the mission of the church is simply to be truly church, to be a community that somehow points to the coming reign of God. But this pointing to the reign is not limited to announcing it verbally. It is also a matter of living it, so that we who are in the church, even in the midst of all our imperfections, may somehow enjoy and offer a foretaste of the future that we expect. This is why divisions, contention, gossip, and politicking within the church have a tragic dimension. When those who approach the church see such things, the mission suffers, witness is weakened, and we give ample reason to those who say that they want nothing to do with such a church. This is why, in the Gospel of John, Jesus asks of the Father "that they may all be one . . . so that the world may believe that you have sent me" (John 17:21).

In any case, one must stress the fact that mission is always turned outwards. Although the inner life of the church is part of its mission as a sign of hope for the world, it is not a matter of having a sacred corner where we can withdraw from the difficulties of the world in order to rejoice in our mutual love. Instead, it's a matter of having this experience of Christian life move us in two parallel directions. The first of these is to witness to the Lord of the church. The second is to discover, acknowledge, and point out the presence of that very Lord in other places around us.

We may begin with the first of these two, which is the best known and discussed. Certainly, the mission of the church includes a witness beyond the church itself. But this is a particular kind of witness, one whose shape has to be determined by its contents. Towards the end of the Gospel of John, after his resurrection, Jesus appears before his disciples and tells them, "As the Father sent me, so I send you" (John 20:21). The mission of the church is based on being sent by this Jesus who was sent by the Father. But let us not forget that Jesus says "as the Father sent me." We are not sent in the same way in which a soap company sends out people to sell its goods, and much less are we sent to proclaim the gospel automatically, in the manner of those impersonal, robotic calls that try to sell us a product or a politician over the phone. We are sent as Jesus was sent. As in his case, this being sent implies being present. Jesus is not a word that God wrote in the clouds, nor a speech that God spoke in the thunder. Jesus is the presence of God in our midst. In Jesus, God doesn't speak to us from afar, but approaches humanity, joins it, walks and suffers with it. Thus, if the church is sent as Jesus was sent, this means that it isn't enough for the church to make powerful declarations, or to have radio and television programs speaking about Jesus. It is necessary for the church to be in the midst of the pains and hopes of humanity, and above all the church must suffer with those who suffer and rejoice with those who rejoice. The church is here not to look at the world from outside and criticize it, but rather to enter the world and through its own presence to give witness to Jesus Christ: he, being in the form of God, did not take this as something to which he must cling, but emptied himself, took the form of a servant, and was made like us (Phil. 2:6–7). If Jesus did not come to be served, but to serve, the church has been created not to be served, or admired, or powerful, but to serve. Without service, whatever mission we have is not the mission of Jesus Christ.

But we must also remember that part of the mission of the church is to discover, acknowledge, and point to the presence of this same Lord in other places around us. Along with the missionary sending in John 20 that we have just discussed, we must remember another, the much better known sending that appears at the end of the Gospel of Matthew, which is commonly called the Great Commission. Many of us have learned the words by heart from our very early steps in the life of faith: "Go therefore and make disciples of all nations, baptizing them in the name of the Father and of the Son and of the Holy Spirit, and teaching them to obey everything that I have commanded you. And remember, I am with you always, to the end of the age" (Matt. 28:19–20). But too often we forget the word "therefore," which implies that the reason why Jesus is telling this to his disciples has just been mentioned. Certainly, we are to go and make disciples. But the reason for this is not that we are to take Jesus to places where he is not present. On the contrary, the reason for our mission is that Jesus is already Lord of all nations.

In the verse immediately before what we call the Great Commission, Jesus says, "All authority in heaven and on earth has been given to me." We are not sent to make him Lord. We are sent because he already is Lord. The mission of the church in Chicago is not taking Jesus to Chicago. The mission of the church in Manchuria is not taking Jesus to Manchuria. Jesus is already Lord, and he is already there, even though this may not be known by unbelievers, by politicians, by merchants—and even though we ourselves often forget it. The mission of the church in Chicago, Manchuria, or Puerto Rico includes discovering, acknowledging, and pointing to the presence of our Lord in these various places around us—including those places where he is ignored, disobeyed, and even despised. When we're able to see the presence of our Lord out there, quite apart from our church and its witness, this helps us to be what we should be: a church that exists not to be served, but to serve. We are here in order to serve a society in which, despite all that could be said about its corrupt politicians, its unscrupulous financiers, and its domestic violence, Jesus is already active. He is acting through the church. But he is also acting in ways that we cannot fathom, quite apart from us and from the church. Therefore, the mission of the church includes discovering the places in which God is already acting in the surrounding society, and joining God in those places.

In summary, there is an inner element of the mission of the church consisting in making sure that the church is the church, that we are a place where one may at least catch a glimpse of the glorious reign that we await. There is another element consisting in announcing to the world around us the grace and love of God that we have known in Jesus Christ by virtue of the Holy Spirit. And there is a third element consisting in discovering, acknowledging, and joining what our Lord is already doing around us even apart from the church or any religious claim. To those who believe in him, the Great Commission reminds us that this Lord who invites us to enjoy now a foretaste of his reign, who commands us to witness to him and to find him in unexpected places in the world around us, will be with us in all those places till the final day.

## For Reflection and Discussion

1. If you invite someone to attend your church and she tells you that she doesn't need a church to be Christian, how do you respond? Is it possible to be a Christian without any relationship to any community of faith? What do you think about Cyprian's affirmation that in order to have God as Father, one must also have the church as mother? What is the value in such a declaration—and what are the dangers?

2. What do we lose if we try to follow Christ without belonging to any church? Why do some people seem to follow that route?

3. If someone asks you what you mean by believing in the church, what would you answer? Do you mean that you will accept whatever the church leaders say? Or does it mean something else?

4. Can a church whose members aren't totally pure say that it is holy? How do you answer someone who tells you that they don't want to join the church because there are too many sinners in it?

5. What sort of divisions do you see in the church today? What should we do about them?

6. Make a list of five words that you consider to be fundamental for the mission of the church. If you're part of a
   group, compare your lists, and discuss the importance
   of each of the words you've suggested.

## SEVEN

# *Worship in the Church*

While it is true that the church lives *for* mission, it is also true that it lives *by* worship. When we come to this point, we must begin by confessing that too often what most divides us from other believers are our various forms of worship. Some worship in one way, and some in another, and each of the two declares that the other form of worship is not truly Christian. We will return to this subject later on; but we must begin by remembering that what is important in worship isn't how we worship, but whom we worship. If the God whom we worship is one, our various forms of worship are all addressed to the same throne. And if the God whom we worship is love, our various forms of worship must also promote and express mutual love.

If we wish to declare that our worship is "biblical," what's most important is not that we copy all the details and customs of the very early church. In fact, such a goal would be impossible, for we no longer speak the same language, or dress the same way, or live under the same conditions.

Besides, the New Testament says little about how worship was conducted in the primitive church. Being "biblical" in worship is having such worship make us the people of God, joined in the mutual love that the Bible requires and sharing the missionary vision that the Bible inspires.

## What Scripture Teaches Us about Worship

Possibly the best way to begin a discussion of worship is to look at the experience of the prophet Isaiah as it appears in chapter 6 of his book. This is a common way in which worship is discussed, and it will be helpful to summarize it here. Isaiah's experience begins with an overwhelming vision of God: "I saw the Lord sitting on a throne, high and lofty; and the hem of his robe filled the temple" (Isa. 6:1). Worship always begins with this acknowledgment of the glory and majesty of God, and is grounded in this acknowledgment. In various churches this is done in different ways—some with calm contemplation, and some with joyous exuberance. In some churches, this acknowledgment is a series of songs that together are often called "praise." In others this is done by singing a "hymn of praise" such as "Holy, Holy, Holy," which points to the majesty, power, and presence of God. In some churches it is customary to begin with biblical words such as "The Lord is in his holy Temple." But no matter how this is done, most churches begin their worship service with the acknowledgment and proclamation of the greatness of this God whom we worship.

Next, Isaiah sees that he is not alone in this vision of God's majesty. Surrounding the throne there are seraphs who sing "Holy, holy, holy is the LORD of hosts; the whole earth is full of his glory" (Isa. 6:3). While in his vision Isaiah relates directly to God, he also knows that he's not alone in his worship. Jointly with him the seraphs sing praises to God, and the entire earth proclaims God's glory.

This shows that, even while in worship we relate personally to God, we don't do this by ourselves, but rather in the company of the rest of the congregation, as well as with the enormous multitude who sing the glory of the same God jointly with us, even though we don't see them. This is why it's important to make certain that in worship we use not only the first-person singular "I," but also the plural "we." This communal and even cosmic mission of worship is expressed in many of our hymns and songs, including the well-known hymn inspired by the vision of Isaiah that is still sung in churches throughout the world: "Holy, Holy, Holy, Lord God Almighty." Whether we sing a traditional hymn such as this or use other words, we must find ways to acknowledge that worship is grounded in the majesty of God, and that it involves not individual praise but communal praise in which we join the entire church through the ages, all of creation, and even angels and archangels.

As we've noted, the Christian faith necessarily has a communal dimension. What we saw regarding Scripture is also true regarding worship: it is good and necessary to praise God privately, on our own; but it is also necessary to praise God as a community. Worshiping the God who is love requires a community of love. Worshiping the triune God, Father, Son, and Holy Spirit, the God in whose very bosom there is a community of love, requires that there also be a community of love among those who worship. Furthermore, if we study the role of worship throughout the Bible, beginning already with the Old Testament, we see that one of the purposes of worship, besides rendering honor to God, is to shape the people of God. This people is not a collection of isolated individuals, each coming to God on his or her own account, but is a single body whom God calls, shapes, and uses: the people of God.

This means that worship must always be a joint action and experience of all worshipers together. Worship is not a show or a spectacle, like a play that moves and inspires us. Nor is it like a modern concert, where people go in order to admire a singer or a band, and then perhaps join them in singing. Nor is it the passive participation expressed in the phrase that I heard frequently from my classmates when I was growing up: "I'm going to hear mass." Worship is a common action of the entire worshiping community. No matter whether one improvises or employs words and formulae written beforehand, worship is never the work of the pastor or of anyone else directing it. Worship happens when the people of God celebrate who God is and what God does for us; it happens when we confess our sins and shortcomings and listen to the commands of God.

Since every community needs coordinated action, worship leaders are important. They are the ones who in many ways determine what is to be done, said, and sung. Without their leadership, chaos would reign. But at the same time, it's important to point out that all who participate in worship are equally worshipers. This includes the preacher, the music leaders, and even the person sitting in the last pew.

Unfortunately, sometimes we forget this to such an extent that in some churches we find worship leaders who declare themselves to be "worshipers," forgetting that they are no more that than anybody else in the congregation. Our worship is the "work of the people."

When we return to the vision of Isaiah, we find that when he sees the glory of God, he immediately sees his own sin as well: "Woe is me! I am lost, for I am a man of unclean lips, and I live among a people of unclean lips; yet my eyes have seen the King, the LORD of hosts!" (Isa. 6:5). The vision of God's glory and majesty, while leading us to praise, also reveals our impurity and sin. We are not worthy to be in the presence of God, and we must acknowledge that. For this reason, one way or another, the vision of the glory of God must bring us to confessing our own sin. Worship leads us not only to the presence of God, but also to a profound sense of this sin that alienates us from God. And, as in the case of Isaiah, we confess not only our own individual sin, but also that of the entire community. Like Isaiah, we are people of unclean lips, and we live among a people of unclean lips.

This is why, from the most ancient times, Christian worship always included a time for confession. In some cases, someone would confess a grave sin before God and the congregation. But most commonly there was a moment in worship in which, after seeing the glory of God, the congregation confessed its sinfulness as a whole. This is still done in many churches today. That common confession reminds us that, just as our worship is not a purely individual matter, neither is our sin purely individual. Of course we commit sins as individuals, and we have to confess that before God.

But sin is also a social and communal reality. Isaiah acknowledges that he lives in the midst of a people of unclean lips. Today we have to acknowledge that our individual sin is part of our collective sin, and that we have to confess before God both our individual sin and that which is collective and social. As we shall see further on, this social and corporate dimension of sin also leads us to a wider view of our mission.

In summary, the very vision of the glory of God leads us to the acknowledgment of our sin, and thus the second essential element of worship, after praise for God's majesty, is a confession of how far we are from God's will for our lives. But we dare to confess our sin before God because, being the people of God, we know God's love and God's will to forgive.

It's becoming increasingly common in some churches to limit worship to praise, with no time for confession. As a result, people who come with a conscience burdened by guilt have no opportunity to present that guilt before God and receive the gift of divine grace. Sometimes, the lack of a time for confession gives the impression that sin isn't such a serious matter after all. If all worship is simply a matter of praising God, there's no reason to change the way we are or how we relate to each other. This allows us to hide the contradiction between praising God and keeping our hatred and resentment against others—often against others who are members of the same church and partake in the same worship.

From praise and confession we turn to acknowledging and receiving the grace of God that cleanses us from sin. This is also reflected in the vision of the prophet when he says that one of the seraphs came to him with a live coal and said, "Now that this has touched your lips, your guilt has departed and your sin is blotted out" (Isa. 6:7). This then leads us to an even more joyful praise and to mutual reconciliation. If God forgives and cleanses us, we also have the obligation to forgive one another. In the ancient church this forgiveness was expressed by means of the kiss of peace. In many churches today, it is expressed by shaking hands or hugging one another in what is usually called "sharing the peace." A fairly common way of inviting this sharing is declaring that, as a people reconciled with God, we must also give one another signs of mutual reconciliation. Sometimes this includes phrases such as "May the Lord bless you" and "May the peace of the Lord be with you." In this way, worship provides the opportunity to show and to experience the truth that being reconciled with God implies and requires also being reconciled with others. If we are children of the same loving Father, we are brothers and sisters among ourselves, and we have to acknowledge that in both worship and our daily dealings.

Isaiah then hears the voice of the Lord say, "Whom shall I send, and who will go for us?" (Isa. 6:8). The vision and forgiveness that Isaiah receives are not only for his own benefit, but also involve his being sent, his mission. The same is true in our case. Worship is not only for our own benefit, but also so that we may hear the voice of God sending us out in mission. This is what often happens in the sermon, in which we are shown that the majesty of the God that we have seen, the sin that we have acknowledged, and the unmerited grace that we have received are not only for our own benefit, but are also intended to send us out into the world in order to proclaim God's majesty and reign over it, in order to make it see its sin, and in order to invite it to experience the same forgiveness and grace that we have received.

We often forget that the New Testament repeatedly refers to the church as a community of "kings and priests" (Rev. 1:6, KJV), a "holy priesthood" (1 Peter 2:5), and a "royal priesthood" (1 Peter 2:9). This is reflected in the phrase "the universal priesthood of believers," which we often employ in our churches. But we must reinterpret and amplify what this phrase means. We are frequently told that the universal priesthood means that we have no need of priests, but are each able to approach the heavenly throne directly. This way of understanding the universal priesthood is partly the result of Protestant polemics against a Roman Catholicism in which priests seemed to control access to God. It is also partly the legacy of recent centuries of extreme individualism, when all that was important was one's individual relationship to God. "Universal priesthood" doesn't mean only that every Christian has direct access to God. It means also and above all that all of us as a priestly body are to take the rest of humankind before the heavenly throne. In very ancient times it was the custom, immediately before celebrating communion, to engage in what was called "the prayer of the faithful." This was a prayer in which the entire church, as a priestly body, prayed both for its own members and for others—including the emperor who persecuted them.

Accordingly, when in the midst of its worship the church prays in intercession for others, it's performing part of its mission, taking the entire creation before God's presence.

This implies that such prayers of intercession should be not only for those who are ill or grieving among our own congregation, but also for the rest of the church wherever it is, as well as for a humankind suffering violence, injustice, and alienation from God.

Christian worship then leads to mission. Since most of that mission takes place after worship, beyond the limits of the church, in everyday life, it is an ancient custom to end the service with words of sending and a benediction. Most commonly, that benediction is also a call on the triune God to walk with believers in their daily life: "The grace of the Lord Jesus Christ, the love of God, and the communion of the Holy Spirit be with all of you" (2 Cor. 13:13).

## Exploring Diversity in Worship

Although the passage of Isaiah that we've just discussed is commonly read and employed in all churches, and all base their worship on experiences similar to those of Isaiah, the worldwide church encompasses an enormous variety of forms of worship. Such variety is due to several reasons. One of them is the diversity of cultures in which faith has become incarnate. There are cultures in which the deepest and most moving experiences are expressed in dance and rhythm; and there are others in which the same experiences, equally deep and moving, are expressed by means of a profound silence. The music in some cultures has rhythms that are stronger than melodies, and in other cultures we find the reverse. By becoming incarnate in that great variety of contexts, Christian faith makes use of those and many other cultural elements to express the same majesty of God, the same sense of sin, the same experience of grace, and the same sense of mission.

To this we can add other reasons for diversity in worship. Some of them have to do with the age of worshipers, for the culture in which we live has evolved so rapidly in recent years that the expressions and tastes of one generation often differ widely from those of the next. Some sociologists claim that in our society there are at least four different generations. They say, for instance, that seniors generally hold respect for authority, while the next generation—the baby boomers—have an ambivalent attitude towards authority. The subsequent generation—Generation X—just isn't terribly interested in the social order and therefore in authority in general. But the most recent generation seems to be more inclined to look upon authority with favor. Such generational differences may be seen also in interpersonal relationships. For instance, while older generations prefer meeting face-to-face, many of the younger generation prefer the so-called social networks.

The impact of all this on the worship of the church is obvious. Older generations, for whom attending a concert means to sit and listen, differ from the younger ones, for whom a concert includes audience participation in singing, shouting, and even "surfing" the crowd.

Other differences in worship reflect social and cultural differences. In a highly stratified society, there are also different levels of education, different social practices, different expressions of courtesy, and so on. All of these factors may be seen in the diversity of worship today.

This is why we said at the beginning of this chapter that, while worship ought to be the center of unity for the church, it actually is one of the places at which our divisions are more visible and profound. Some people even speak of "worship wars," in which congregations divide into two groups because of their conflicting feelings about worship. What do we do about that? Certainly we can't expect or demand that people worship in ways that are alien to their own experience and culture. Worship has to relate to the conditions of our life, to touch the deepest fibers of our being. Precisely because we are a multitude that no one can count, from every people, language, tribe, and nation, our worship will be varied, and any effort to reach uniform and universal practices will necessarily fail. Throughout its entire history, even during times of greatest uniformity, the church has never worshiped in a single, uniform, and universal way.

But there are some things that we can do. First of all, we can acknowledge that all of our forms of worship reflect not only what we find in Scripture, but also our various cultures, tastes, ages, and so on. So, even though I may prefer a particular form of worship, I may not undervalue other forms that others find more significant. If a certain type of music helps me to express God's majesty, to acknowledge my sin, and to go out into the world to serve God, I should not and cannot criticize those who employ another kind of music for the same purpose and the same results. In short, the first thing we must do is to acknowledge one another as members of a single church of Jesus Christ that worships in a multitude of forms and languages, and seeks to incarnate the faith in an enormous variety of cultures and experiences.

Second, I must acknowledge that worship is not primarily for me. Worship is first of all for God; second, it is for the worshiping community; and only as a distant third is it for me as an individual. Thus, if at any point during a worship service a certain song or gesture isn't to my liking—or, as we frequently say, "doesn't speak to me"—this doesn't mean that it's out of place in worship. Next to me there may be sisters and brothers for whom what is being said or done is enormously significant. Let me offer a case in point.

Some years ago in a congregation that included people who spoke English, Spanish, and Vietnamese, the three groups decided to have meetings in which they would try to come to understand one another better by sharing their deepest experiences. In one of those meetings, an elderly Vietnamese man said that a particular song that was traditionally part of every service—the *Gloria*—was his favorite, because this is what the congregation of his childhood was singing when armed men broke into the church and took away his father, whom he never saw again. In response to that witness, someone asked him to teach the Vietnamese words of the song to the rest of the congregation. From that point on, that hymn, sung in Vietnamese by the entire congregation, composed mostly of people who didn't understand a word of what they were saying (but knew the general meaning), came to have profound significance for the entire church. The hymn became particularly valuable not because all who sang it understood the words, but because they understood something of the emotions that it evoked in one of the brothers singing with them.

This may serve as an example to follow in situations that may not be as dramatic, but are just as real when a particular group prefers one sort of music and some prefer another. If worship is not for me or mine, but is actually the worship of the entire community, as part of that community I must make every effort to understand and share the emotions and experiences of my brothers and sisters in the faith. If at some point an element in worship "doesn't speak to me," I can at least try to hear what it says to those who are worshiping with me. Likewise, I expect that when something in worship says nothing to them but is important to me, they too will try to understand why it is so.

We must also realize that quite often the differences between one form of worship and another are not as great as we imagine. For instance, in a more traditional type of worship the person presiding says, "The Lord be with you," and the congregation responds, "And with your spirit"; and in what seems a radically different service the person presiding says, "Good morning. May God bless you," and the congregation responds, "Good morning." Some leaders say, "Let us give thanks to the Lord," to which the congregation responds, "It is meet and right so to do," while in other churches the leader says, "God is good," and the congregation responds, "All the time." While one of these is more traditional and the other makes use of more common language, both are saying the same thing. And the same is true at many other points in a worship service. Some say, "Lift up your hearts," and others say, "Let's lift up our hands."

Some say, "The peace of our Lord Jesus Christ be with you," and others say, "May the Lord bless you." As we analyze such practices, we realize that the difference is not as profound as we imagine, but that these are simply different ways of expressing similar feelings and experiences.

In all of this, it is important for us to understand that mission doesn't take place only outside the church building, for the worship of the church is part of its mission. This is so, first, because worship itself is a proclamation of the presence of God in the believing community and of God's love for it. And this is so because an essential element in mission is that reconciliation which we celebrate and express in worship itself. Finally, this is so because mission also includes intercessory prayer, the priestly task of interceding not only for the church and its members, but also for the entire creation of God.

*             *             *

In this chapter we have focused our attention on worship in general. But there are two important rites that the church has celebrated throughout the centuries and still celebrates today as essential parts of worship. These are baptism and communion, which we will discuss in the next chapter.

### For Reflection and Discussion

1. Why is it that worship so often divides us instead of uniting us? In your local church, are there debates and

even dissension about worship and what ought to be done in it? What can you do to help solve those differences and at the same time make it possible for all to share equally in worship?

2. What is your attitude when something is done in worship that you don't like but that other people consider important? How might you change your attitude?

3. Review the various elements of worship discussed in this chapter on the basis of Isaiah's vision. Compare them with worship in your church. Do we tend to forget some of the elements mentioned here? How can we restore them to our worship?

4. Have you met people who specialize in leading worship and express this role by calling themselves "worshipers"? To what extent is this proper? What are the values and the dangers in such titles?

5. When we speak of a liturgy, usually we refer to a specific way of worshiping, with certain set rites, words, and symbols. If "liturgy" is the way in which people render honor to God and listen to God's Word, can there be a worship service that is not somehow liturgical? When you hear the word "liturgy," is your response generally positive or negative? Why?

# EIGHT

# Baptism and Communion

From the earliest times in the life of the church, there were two rites or practices that had a crucial role in that life: baptism and communion. These are generally known as "sacraments" or "ordinances." Some churches prefer the first of these two terms, "sacraments." In the words of St. Augustine, a sacrament is "an external and visible sign of an inner and invisible grace." Others prefer to speak of these rites as "ordinances," pointing out that it was Christ who ordered them. Generally, those who prefer the first of these two words stress the action of God in baptism and communion, while those who prefer the second see them rather as symbolic actions representing believers' repentance and commitments. We will return to this later on.

Although almost all Protestant denominations speak of these two practices as either "sacraments" or "ordinances," some are not in agreement with this. The best-known are the Quakers or Friends and the Salvation Army. The Quakers arose in the seventeenth century as a group of believers reacting against what they felt was the excessive formalism and insufficient substance in Christian worship. The endless debates about the manner in which Christ is present in communion seemed to deny the very essence of communion, which is a spirit of love. In response to this, Quakers hold that both true baptism and true communion are inner and invisible realities that have no need of external means such as the water of baptism and the bread and wine of communion.

The Salvation Army, which arose in the nineteenth century, doesn't practice baptism or communion for reasons similar to those of the Quakers. A further reason was that at that time women weren't allowed to preside in communion, and from its very beginning the Salvation Army insisted on the absolute equality between men and women. If women weren't allowed to preside over the sacrament, men shouldn't do it, either. Also, since this organization frequently worked among people addicted to alcohol, it feared that the wine of communion would lead some of them back to their addiction. At any rate, it's important to point out that the Salvation Army isn't opposed to the sacraments themselves, and doesn't object to one of its members being baptized or receiving communion in another church.

While most Protestant denominations count only baptism and communion among the sacraments or ordinances, some add the washing of feet, following the words of Jesus in John 13:14–17. Many others, while practicing foot-washing on certain occasions, don't consider it a sacrament or an ordinance such as baptism and communion. As for Roman Catholicism, it affirms that there are seven sacraments: baptism, confirmation, communion, penance, marriage, ordination, and the anointing of the sick. Historically, one may say that in ancient times, while baptism and communion had particular importance, there were many other practices that were sometimes called "sacraments." It wasn't until the twelfth century, mainly through the influential four books of *Sentences* by Peter Lombard, that the number of the sacraments was fixed as seven. In the Orthodox tradition (churches such as the Greek Orthodox Church and the Russian Orthodox Church), the most common practice is, as in antiquity, to stress particularly baptism and communion, but also to call many other rites and practices "mysteries"— which is the manner in which those churches refer to the sacraments.

To sum up: the vast majority of Christian churches see baptism and communion as particularly important, usually considering baptism to be the initiation into Christian life.

## Disagreements about Baptism

As is well known, there are wide disagreements about baptism among various Protestant traditions. These disagreements have to do with the way in which baptism is to be administered and also with the age at which people may receive it. Let us look at these two issues in order.

First, there is the matter of how baptism is to be administered. The references in the New Testament indicate that baptism is a sign of the death and new life of the believer grounded in the death and resurrection of Jesus Christ. This doesn't leave much room to doubt that in very early times, baptism by immersion was the most common—for just as Jesus descended to the tomb and came out of it, so the person being baptized enters the water and rises out of it. But apparently other forms of baptism were also permitted when circumstances required it. Thus, the *Didache* or *Doctrine of the Twelve Apostles*, a document that was apparently written late in the first century, when the New Testament was still incomplete, instructs that baptism is to be done in "living water"—that is, running water. Still, it makes allowances: If there is no running water, baptism may be done in still water, and if even such water isn't available, baptism may be administered by pouring water over the head three times, in the name of the Father, the Son, and the Holy Spirit. Additionally, the most ancient baptistry that has been found is of such a size that it would be difficult to submerge a person completely in it. This, as well as other indications, leads to the conclusion that one way of baptizing was to have the candidate enter the water and kneel in it, and then have water poured over his or her head. To this day, the most common practice in the Eastern churches is to baptize children by immersion, and to baptize adults by having them kneel in the baptismal pool and pouring water on their heads.

In the Western church—that is, the Latin-speaking church from which both Roman Catholicism and Protestantism have sprung—the same practice was followed for a long time. In Rome, children were still baptized by immersion in the eleventh century. (Apparently, one reason for the change was that as Christianity expanded to the colder lands in the north, it became more difficult and perhaps even harmful to baptize children by immersion.) Today, some Protestants insist that the only valid baptism is by immersion, and that those who have been baptized in a different way have to be re-baptized. Others baptize by immersion, but receive those who have been baptized in a different manner. Among those churches that baptize by pouring or sprinkling water on the head of the candidate, almost all accept baptism by immersion as well.

In any case, it's important to note that the most consequential differences pertain not to the manner of baptism, but rather to the age and condition of the person to be baptized. This may be suggested in certain sixteenth-century practices: the first Anabaptists did not originally baptize by immersion; it was later that they began insisting on it.

The matter of the age of those receiving baptism is much more important, because it is the result of different views on baptism itself. This issue becomes particularly difficult to resolve because, despite all the arguments each side has adduced to prove its point, the New Testament does not in fact speak clearly on the matter. It neither mentions nor prohibits infant baptism. Around the year 200, Tertullian wrote against infant baptism, but his reason for it was very different from what we hear today. He thought that baptism granted an unrepeatable amnesty from all previous sins, and that therefore it was to be postponed until all the sins of youth were behind the candidate. In the third century, in his detailed instructions about how to administer baptism, Hippolytus takes for granted that among those receiving the rite were children so young that they were incapable of responding to the questions posed to them, and their parents would answer in their stead. In short, historical studies, although offering some useful hints, don't resolve the matter.

At the time of the Reformation, some began rejecting the practice of infant baptism because it seemed to imply that the mere fact of having been born in a supposedly Christian society made one a Christian. This made the church practically coextensive with the society at large, for those belonging to that society also belonged to the church. It was typical of a time when churches were state churches, and thus it was expected that everyone born within a state would follow its religion. The early Anabaptists rejected infant baptism because they were convinced that there is a vast difference between the church and society at large, and that belonging to the latter doesn't guarantee belonging to the former. For the same reason, in more recent times some theologians from churches that have traditionally baptized infants have raised objections to that practice, not on the basis of whether such baptism is valid or not, but on the basis that, in the context of an ever more secularized society, the church must make it very clear that one does not become a believer by the mere fact of being part of society.

Today, the reason most commonly cited against infant baptism is quite different: that baptism is a sign of repentance and conversion, which an infant can neither do nor understand. This is an important point, because God's grace requires our acceptance, and, as we have already pointed out, there's a close relationship between faith and understanding. On the other hand, we must be careful not to take this argument too far, because if we were to wait until we understood all that baptism is and means before receiving it, we would never be baptized. The action of God's grace in baptism, as well as in faith itself and in conversion, is always a mystery that our minds will never understand. This becomes an important matter as the population in our society ages, and there are increasing numbers of senior people whose memory and mind fail. Does this mean that their baptism now means nothing because they no longer understand it? Certainly not! But, even so, arguments favoring adult baptism are strong, and those who insist on it testify to the entire church that faith has to be a matter of personal decision and commitment, and that the church isn't the same as a the society around it, even when that society calls itself Christian.

The most common argument defending infant baptism is also the weakest: that the church has practiced it for many centuries—perhaps even beginning during the time of the New Testament. Since the New Testament itself gives no instructions on the matter, those who believe that traditional practices should be continued as long as they don't contradict Scripture simply continue doing what has been done before. The strongest argument for infant baptism is that baptism itself is a sign of the absolutely free grace of God. Baptizing an infant who obviously has done nothing to merit that grace reminds all of us that in salvation the focus must always be on the loving grace of God, and not on our own works or anything we might do, believe, or declare. Professing the faith is a matter of central importance for Christian life, but that very profession has to begin by declaring that what we are and what we believe are above all gifts of the grace of God. At the same time, even in those churches that have traditionally baptized infants, there is a growing insistence that baptism is not simply a nice rite applied to babies, but is grounded in the confession of faith of the congregation as well as the parents and grandparents, and in their commitment to guide the child being baptized along the same path of faith.

In summary, while the practice of baptizing adults only is a witness before the entire church to the need to accept the grace of God in an active and committed manner, the practice of infant baptism is a witness to the primacy of grace in salvation. Both are true, and the church certainly needs both witnesses.

On this matter, as in so many others, both of these positions warn us of the danger of falling into extremes that deny fundamental elements in Christian faith. Those who baptize infants remind the entire church of the primacy of grace. Those who refuse to do it remind the entire church of the need for the will to receive the grace of God. When in Ephesians 4 we read of the "one baptism," this doesn't mean baptism practiced by others in exactly the same fashion; it means a baptism that is one because it makes us part of the one body of Christ, thanks to the one Spirit, and makes us participants in the one hope. As the text itself says, when it comes to this matter, as in so many others, we must act "with all humility and gentleness, with patience, bearing with one another in love, making every effort to maintain the unity of the Spirit in the bond of peace" (Eph. 4:2–3). It is in response to the one Spirit and the one Lord, and not thanks to our agreement among ourselves, that we have "one hope" (v. 4) in our calling, and "one God and Father of all" (v. 6).

## What Baptism Means

What, then, is the meaning of baptism? The answer is that baptism has many different meanings that are not mutually contradictory, but complementary.

First, baptism—particularly adult baptism—is a witness to our faith. Normally, as part of the baptismal rite, the person being baptized makes a public declaration of faith. (In the churches that baptize infants, a public declaration of faith is also required, although in this case the parents and others who are to raise the child make that declaration.)

But baptism is also an affirmation of the primacy of the grace of God. In baptism we use water just as it comes from nature. Water isn't the result of human effort or work—it's a free gift from God. In this way, baptism reminds us that the same God who brings rain upon us and gives us water is the one whose grace rains on God's people.

Baptism is also an action of the entire church that receives a new member into the body and makes itself responsible for him or her. This is why most Protestant denominations insist that baptism take place in the presence of the congregation, and not in private. In baptism, those who receive it make vows of faithfulness to God. And the church administering it, while renewing the vows made at the baptism of each of its members, also vows to accompany the newly baptized in their pilgrimage of faith.

In the ancient church, people often referred to the "seal of baptism." Just as a slave was branded with the seal of his master, so in baptism we are marked with the seal of our Lord. In baptism, by the grace of God, we are no longer servants of evil because we have become servants of Christ. Another way of expressing this in today's terms would be to speak of baptism as the certification of a new citizenship. Today we frequently see "naturalization" ceremonies in which people acquire a new citizenship. Something similar happens in baptism, for, as Paul says, "our citizenship is in heaven" (Phil. 3:20).

The Scriptures often refer also to the "cleansing" of baptism. This image means that in baptism, by the grace of God and through faith, we are cleansed from sin. This is a powerful image, particularly for those who come to baptism with a strong sense of having been made dirty by sin. At the same time, however, it is important not to allow baptism to be seen as a sort of amnesty by which previous sins are forgiven, with the consequence that sins committed after baptism need some other form of cleansing. This is what happened in the medieval church, and it eventually led to the sale of indulgences, against which Luther and many others protested.

For this reason it is important to keep in mind another image or way of understanding baptism: to see it as a grafting into Christ and his body. The basis for this image is found in John 15, where Jesus says that he is the true vine and we are the branches. The branch is grafted into the vine and lives by virtue of that grafting, through which the life of the vine comes to it. A grafting is valid not only when it is done, but continues as long as the branch is part of the vine. Likewise, baptism is not only the beginning of Christian life, but the very fact of being baptized is the basic reality that makes us who we are as believers.

Catholic theologian Karl Rahner reminds us that we begin to die at baptism, and that the new birth of baptism is finally fulfilled in our physical death. This relationship between the death and resurrection of Christ on the one hand, and the death and new birth of the believer on the other, was expressed in the ancient church through the custom of celebrating most baptisms early on Easter morning.

## Different Beliefs about Communion

As we turn our attention to communion, we will see that communion, like baptism, has created significant differences among various Christian denominations. Some of these have to do with the manner in which communion is celebrated: in some churches believers remain seated while the bread and wine are taken to them, while in others every believer goes forward and kneels. Some use wine, and others grape juice; some use bread, and others wafers. But all of these differences are minor when compared to the great debates that have arisen about the very meaning of communion and the manner in which Christ is present in it. Some of those differences may be described in a fairly simple manner. The Roman Catholic Church subscribes to the doctrine of transubstantiation, which teaches that in the very act of consecration, bread and wine are no longer those things but become the body and blood of Christ in the appearance of bread and wine. Most of the Lutheran tradition holds that, while the bread and wine are still such, they are also the body and blood of Jesus Christ. This is sometimes called the doctrine of "consubstantiation." Many other churches hold that communion is essentially a symbolic act reminding us of the death and resurrection of Jesus. The result of these debates is the tragedy that communion, which should be the link of unity among all believers, has become one of our main causes of division and acrimony. Partly for that reason, John Calvin sought to leave aside such debates, arguing that what is important is not that Christ comes to the table of communion, but rather that in the very celebration, by the power of the Holy Spirit, the congregation is taken into heaven, where Jesus is seated at the right hand of God, in order to enjoy a foretaste of the final banquet.

Without claiming to have solved such debates, today we center our attention on other dimensions of communion that have frequently been forgotten or eclipsed. The first of them is the relationship between communion and the spirit of love and justice that must reign among believers. This may be seen in the well-known passage of Paul in his first epistle to the Corinthians, chapter 11, where we read, among other things, that "all who eat and drink without discerning the body, eat and drink judgment against themselves" (11:29). We frequently imagine that these words refer to the manner in which we understand the presence of Christ in the bread and wine, or that they refer to the feelings and attitudes with which we come to the table, or even to our lack of devotion. But if we read the entire passage, we see that what worries Paul is not the doctrinal question of how Jesus is present in communion, but rather that believers in Corinth, instead of seeing the Supper as a true occasion for love and community, have twisted it in such a way that some have too much to eat and drink, while others go hungry. That is why Paul admonishes them by saying, "When you come together, it is not really to eat the Lord's supper" (11:20). When we read the entire context, what Paul says about not discerning the body of the Lord seems to refer not so much to the bread itself as to the gathered community, the church, which is the body of Christ. Those who eat and drink in an unworthy manner are those whose very participation in communion is a rejection of the spirit of love and justice that must exist in the church as the body of Christ.

This takes us to another dimension of communion that for various reasons has often been set aside. That dimension is the celebratory character of communion itself. When we misunderstand the words of Paul just quoted, we tend to think that to eat and drink in a worthy manner means to do so in a profound spirit of compunction and grief for our sin. This is the result of a centuries-long process that slowly eroded the original joy and celebratory spirit of communion and turned it into an austere and even funereal rite. But in the early church what was specifically commemorated in communion was not so much the crucifixion of Jesus as his resurrection. Naturally, what makes the resurrection important is that the crucifixion takes place before it. Yet the last word belongs not to the cross, but to the empty tomb. This is why from the very beginning Christians gathered to break bread particularly on the first day of the week. They did so because the first day of the week was the day of resurrection. (At the same time, one must point out that by gathering on the first day of the week or "Lord's Day," those believers were not rejecting the Sabbath on the seventh day, or trying to substitute for it with Sunday. On the contrary, for some time Christians of Jewish origins, as well as those Gentiles who were able to do so, continued observing the Sabbath as a day of rest. But the specific day to gather and celebrate communion was the first day of the week, the day of the resurrection of Jesus.) In a way, each week commemorated the events of the first Holy Week, so that Friday, the day of the crucifixion, was also a day of fasting and repentance, while the first day of the week, the day of the resurrection, was a time of celebration. Furthermore, since creation began the first day of the week in the Genesis narrative, in communion the church celebrated both the first creation and the second, which began with the resurrection of Jesus. The celebration of communion was also a foretaste of the final banquet, of the day of consummation, when the apparently endless cycle of weeks will end, and eternity will dawn.

All of this made communion a celebration. This is why today, even in churches where communion is most austere and sober, one still speaks of "celebrating" communion. Furthermore, in recent decades, partly due to a rediscovery of ancient worship practices in the church, many churches have returned to the true celebratory character of communion. This may be seen particularly in the words that some churches employ in their ritual books. Thus, for instance, in churches where some fifty years ago the invitation to communion began with the words "All ye who do truly and earnestly repent of your sin . . . ," the new rituals begin with the declaration "This is the joyful feast of the people of God."

## What Communion Means

What can we say about the meaning of communion? We must begin by saying that communion—like all of worship—is analogous to the sustenance that a branch receives from the vine into which it is grafted. The graft itself—in this case, baptism—is always valid, but it also requires that there be a nurturing that only the vine can give it. Those of us who are members of the body of Christ through baptism and confession of faith need to be nurtured constantly so that we may continue living as part of that body. This is why, while baptism is not repeated, communion is, just as the act of grafting into a vine is not repeated, but the ongoing nurturing of the branch by the vine is still necessary.

Communion is also a celebration of gratitude for all of God's gifts. This is why it is often called "eucharist," from a Greek word meaning an act of thanksgiving. In the Gospels, when Jesus instituted the Supper, he "gave thanks." Therefore, communion is a thanksgiving or eucharist that we celebrate in gratitude for all the gifts of the first creation that surround us and feed us, and also for the gifts of the new creation that are a promise of eternal life.

Finally, communion is a celebration of our unity as members of the body of Christ. As Paul says, "Because there is one bread, we who are many are one body, for we all partake of the one bread" (1 Cor. 10:17). We frequently forget the importance of sharing bread and other food as a sign of hospitality and unity. Our English word "to accompany" originally meant breaking bread together. In communion, in breaking bread together, we declare ourselves companions of one another, and at the same time, we celebrate the fact that Christ, whose bread we share, has come to be our companion.

From this follows another important point. In comparing the water of baptism with the bread and wine of communion, we see that, while water is used just as God provides it, bread and wine require human participation in their making. It is through human labor that wheat becomes bread and grapes become wine. Thus, in declaring that, in Christ, God has become our companion, we are also affirming that our work can and must contribute to the work of God. This is why, while there are no ceremonies or words with which we present the water for baptism to God, there is in communion an act of offering to God the bread and wine that we are about to share. (Even though today we frequently use the word "offertory" to refer to the act of collecting offerings, originally, and still in many churches, this word referred to presenting God with the wine and bread for communion, which could also be accompanied by other offerings.)

When people go to the front of the church and sometimes kneel in order to partake of communion, they're declaring themselves to be part of this offering presented to God. And when in some other celebrations people remain seated and all eat the bread and drink the wine at the same time, what is being stressed is the unity of the body of Christ. Thus, communion is both a celebration of unity among believers and an opportunity to renew and reaffirm the vows of our baptism.

Communion is a sign and a celebration of hope. By celebrating it on the eighth day of the week—which is also the first—ancient Christians remembered the final banquet and the eternal life that had been promised to them. By taking bread, they anticipated the day when, like wheat scattered over the fields and hills, the church of Christ in all the corners of the earth would be gathered into a single loaf. This reminder of the future may be seen also in the words of Paul when he says that in celebrating communion we announce the death of the Lord "until he comes" (1 Cor. 11:26).

Finally, whenever we think about baptism and communion, we must remember and insist that they both have their value because of their connection with the very heart of the gospel, the death and resurrection of Jesus Christ.

## For Reflection and Discussion

1. If your church practices infant baptism, what values do you see in that practice? What values do you see in the practice of baptizing adults? Is it possible that somehow each of these two practices witnesses to something important?

2. If your church practices only adult baptism, what values do you see in that practice? What values do you see in the practice of baptizing infants? Is it possible that somehow each of these two practices witnesses to something important?

3. Can you explain why baptism is not to be repeated, while communion is celebrated and repeated regularly?

4. We know that in the ancient church, communion was celebrated at least every week. Why is it that now in many of our churches it is seldom celebrated? Should we celebrate it more often? If so, why? If not, why not?

5. In different churches, communion is celebrated and distributed in various ways. In some, believers go to the front of the church; in some, they remain seated; in some, they stand in a circle; and so on. Review the various forms that you have seen and that you have heard of, and try to understand their meaning. Would it be good to celebrate communion sometimes in one way and sometimes in another? If so, why? If not, why not?

# NINE

# Christian Hope and the Last Days

Much is said today about the "last days" or, to employ traditional terminology, eschatology. All you have to do is turn on your TV set or go to the Internet to find someone who can tell you the exact date and even the exact time when the Lord will come, how present events are the fulfillment of ancient prophecies, who the apocalyptic beast is, and what coming disaster will mark the end of all time. This shouldn't surprise us, because often in past times there were many who devoted years to such reckonings and speculations— and they were all mistaken.

The first thing to be said here is that even though many may claim to base their ideas about the end time on biblical calculations, these notions are actually contradictions of the Bible itself and of what Jesus said. When, at the time of his ascension, the disciples asked him whether the time had come to restore the kingdom to Israel, Jesus told them, "It is not for you to know the times or periods that the Father has set by his own authority" (Acts 1:7). And the same is affirmed elsewhere in the Gospels—for instance, when Jesus says, "But about that day or hour no one knows, neither the angels in heaven, nor the Son, but only the Father. Beware, keep alert; for you do not know when the time will come" (Mark 13:32–33). Therefore, anyone who claims to tell us exactly when the end time will come is claiming to know more than the angels, more than even Jesus himself.

### Preparing for the Last Days with Hope

The Bible speaks not about when the end will come, but rather about how to prepare for it. We're told that we should always be ready for such a moment, precisely because we cannot know the day or the time. Actually, our desire to find out exactly when the end will come is related to our sinful rebellion, because it implies that we don't have to be obedient until the end approaches, and that the only reason for our obedience is that we believe that the end is at hand.

Furthermore, when speaking of the end time or of eschatology, we often commit another serious error. This happens when we turn eschatology into a matter of fear, not of hope. Even the book of Revelation, where we see scenes of great destruction, is actually a book of joy and hope. In that book John addressed the churches in Asia Minor that were facing serious difficulties and were therefore tempted to despair. To reassure them, he sent them a message of hope. When he speaks of the evil to come, he does this not to frighten them, but rather to assure them that their hope is not in vain, and that despite present opposition, in the end those who remain faithful will receive the crown of life. This is why, after the Psalms, the book of Revelation has inspired more hymns than any other book in the Bible. But this book that was originally intended to provide hope is now used to produce fright before the evils to come. This wrongly skews Christian eschatology, which is grounded not on terror but on hope for the final victory of God and of God's purposes for creation.

But "hope" is an ambiguous word. If I say "I hope you're right," what I really mean is that I'm afraid you may be mistaken. If I say "I hope it won't rain on our picnic," what I really mean is that I don't want rain, but I know there's nothing I can do about it. If I say "I hope to finish this task before sundown," what I mean is that I'll try my best to do so. We have to confess that too often our faith is limited to these kinds of hope. We hope that what God says is true. We hope that God will do what we wish. We hope that God will allow us to do what we think we must do.

All of these sorts of hope fall short when we're speaking of Christian hope. Christian hope isn't a mere wish or a possibility, but a certitude. The future for which we wait is as certain and inescapable as the past that we remember—with the enormous difference that quite frequently that past is a cause of shame and compunction, while the future that we await is a reason to rejoice. Once again, Christian eschatology is not about fear, but about hope.

There is also a tendency, when dealing with eschatology, to focus attention on a series of questions that are more a matter of curiosity than anything else and that, no matter how intriguing, are of lesser importance. For instance, people often wonder whether in the future life we will know one another, whether we will completely forget our life of sin, and other similar matters. This is nothing new; it was also a concern among some Christians in ancient times. Apparently some believers in the city of Corinth posed similar questions to Paul: "How are the dead raised? With what kind of body do they come?" (1 Cor. 15:35). Paul answers with the example of a seed, which after being planted produces a body that is quite different from what was planted. In the end, Paul's answer is that it will be God who will determine what sort of bodies there will be, for "God gives it a body as he has chosen, and to each kind of seed its own body" (1 Cor. 15:38). This means that "it is sown a physical body, it is raised a spiritual body" (1 Cor. 15:44). In other words, just as now there are bodies for humans, bodies for fish, and bodies for birds, there will also be a new body that Paul calls a "spiritual body." But Paul doesn't go any further, nor does he claim to know the nature of such a body. Rather, he is content with knowing that God gives each a body as God wishes, and then trusting in the love of this God who will give us much better bodies than we could ever imagine.

### Our Starting Point: God's Love

What all this means—what we must not forget—is that the starting point for eschatology is not our curiosity, but rather God's love. The fundamental eschatological doctrine is the final triumph of God's love and grace. In this context we must remember what was said above: that even though, for us, justice and love frequently seem to be polar opposites, in God these two are intricately connected, in such a way that even when God is doing justice, God is love. This means that we are not to imagine that in the end God loves those who go into eternal life and hates the rest. In a manner that we are quite unable to understand, even in doing justice God is love. This is why eschatology, far from being a matter of fear and trembling, is the surprising and welcome news that the love of God is such that in the end it will prove triumphant and will be forever with us.

Most importantly, even though it has these wonderfully mysterious dimensions that our minds cannot penetrate, eschatological hope has significant consequences not only for the future, but also for the present life of each believer and of the church as a whole. Although we frequently forget it, we actually order our lives and our actions not only on the basis of the past, but also and above all on the basis of the future that we anticipate. We see this even in the simplest decisions of everyday life. When I leave my house, I decide whether to turn right or left not on the basis of where I'm coming from, but rather on the basis of where I want to go. When I go to the market and get a pound of rice, I buy it because I expect to cook it at some point. When I'm sitting here writing these lines, I'm doing so in the hope that you will read them.

This in turn means that the degree to which we truly hope is measured in the decisions that we make on the basis of what we expect. If I tell someone that I'm going to a place that's north, but after leaving my house I turn south, the longer I continue in that direction, the less credible my announced intentions will be. If a friend tells us that when he retires he'll go live in a quiet place in the mountains and spend all his time fishing and looking at sunsets, but now he spends all his time working on a noisy motorcycle and then riding around in the company of other noisy friends, we have reason to doubt that when he retires, he'll do what he says—and if he does, he won't be very happy. If a young woman tells us that when she grows up she'll be a doctor, but she doesn't study now, we have reason to doubt that she really hopes to be a doctor. Likewise, if the church and its members say that we await a reign of love, peace, and justice, our witness will be credible to the extent that we now live practicing and working for love, peace, and justice. If we don't do this, we'll be as believable as I am when I say that I'm going north but constantly drive southward.

This is why the way in which we understand Christian hope is enormously important. For instance, there's a widespread notion that the best way to think of eternal life is as a place where each one of us will have a private cloud, and we'll live without anyone else interrupting our pleasure. But this is very far from the images the Bible uses to describe the future that God promises. The two main images that the Bible employs are the Kingdom of God and the New Jerusalem. Both a kingdom and a city are social realities. A king is good when he rules his kingdom in such a way that his people enjoy relationships of harmony and justice. The word in the book of Revelation that is translated as "city" isn't just an urban reality, but an entire system of government, a political and social order. In other words, when the Bible speaks of the Kingdom or the City of God, it is using communal images rather than those of individual joy. This is why, as already stated, those who have sought to be better Christians by withdrawing from society have discovered that Christian life is, by definition, life in community. This is true because we humans weren't made to be alone, but rather to live in a community of love patterned after the image of the community that exists in the Trinity. Thus, if we truly believe in the promised Kingdom of God or the City of God, we should do everything possible to live now in community and mutual love.

### Being Champions of Peace and Justice

The biblical images of the characteristics of that city and that kingdom may well serve as good guidelines for our present life. Those characteristics are love, peace, and justice. There are countless biblical passages pointing in this direction. One of the best-known descriptions of peace is found in the words of the prophet Micah: "[God] shall judge between many peoples, and shall arbitrate between strong nations far away; they shall beat their swords into plowshares, and their spears into pruning hooks; nation shall not lift up sword against nation, neither shall they learn war any more" (Mic. 4:3). Micah doesn't say this because he's unaware of the war and violence that seem to rule the world. On the contrary, in his book he makes abundant references to the horrible conditions of his time. And it is precisely in the face of such conditions that he proclaims his announcement of hope, of a time when no nation will make war on another.

At this point, however, a word of warning is in order. It's very easy to believe that any condition in which there is no war or open violence is peaceful, even while the violence of injustice remains. We must understand clearly that when the Bible speaks of justice, it isn't referring simply to the process by which laws and courts punish evildoers. On the contrary, it refers most often to justice as a social order in which all have what they need, and there is no abuse or exploitation. This is why, immediately after announcing peace, the prophet also announces, "They shall sit under their own vines and under their own fig trees, and no one shall make them afraid" (Mic. 4:4). It is of this kind of justice that the prophets repeatedly speak. The words of Amos to that effect are well known. The same theme appears repeatedly in the pronouncements of other prophets, including those of Micah himself, who has harsh words for those who oppress others by taking their fields and homes (Mic. 2:1–2). Jesus is also referring to this when he says that we are to seek first of all the reign of God and its justice or righteousness (Matt. 6:33).

All of this means that the peace that has been promised is one without abuse, privilege, or exploitation. Therefore, if we are to live as those who truly expect such a peace, we must now do everything within our reach to seek such a peace that also involves justice. Eschatological hope calls us to live in peace with our neighbors, to increase the sense of community in the church, and to work for peace in society at large. But at the same time we must take care lest that peace, being misunderstood, may lead us to support and defend the violence that the weak constantly suffer.

Here I'm referring not only to the great political debates around elections and economic conflicts within society; I'm also including our life at home. When we think about domestic violence, it's clear that such violence cannot be stopped unless there is also love and justice within the family. Otherwise, what often happens is that a supposed peace is established that is actually a matter of subjection to the more powerful, and therefore is simply another form of abuse and violence. In some cases, domestic violence is kept at bay by fear of the authorities beyond the family itself. When that happens, the problem of violence isn't resolved, but simply hides and finds other means of expression. In neither case is there true peace in the home. The peace that the prophets announce and that believers await and must seek is a peace with justice. Our goal must be the vision of the psalmist: "Righteousness and peace will kiss each other" (Ps. 85:10).

And yet, the peace that the prophets announced goes even further. It is also peace in all of creation and peace between human beings and creation itself. In our earlier discussion of the presence of God in nature, I had to point out that this should not hide the violence that exists in nature. The butterfly is eaten by the bird, and the bird is eaten by the cat. From the viewpoint of our present situation and our past experience, we see no other alternative. But the prophet Isaiah announces a future peace such as we cannot even conceive: "The wolf shall live with the lamb, the leopard shall lie down with the kid, the calf and the lion and the fatling together, and a little child shall lead them" (Isa. 11:6). Obviously, this is poetry, and not an actual description; but even so, it's quite a promise!

Such an outstanding vision destroys any illusions we might have about being able to bring in the reign of God. Just as the ways of God are far above ours, so the designs of God are far above our capabilities. But this doesn't mean that they're not important for our present life. On the contrary, they tell us much about how we are to live today. Just as the promise of peace and justice invites us and demands of us that we live on this earth as those who truly know that peace and justice shall overcome, so the promise of Isaiah calls us to live as those who truly believe that violence has no place in God's final purposes. If it is impossible for us to stop the violence of the wolf against the lamb, or of the leopard against the kid, we can restrain our own violence against one another and against the rest of creation. Just as the fact that others practice injustice and make us unable to end all oppression in the world doesn't exempt us from our obligation to work for justice, so the fact that the wolf violently attacks the lamb doesn't give us license to practice violence against either the wolf or the lamb. According to Isaiah's vision, "a little child shall lead them." It is difficult to imagine a more beautiful way to point to the harmony that is intended between humankind and the rest of creation.

This means that Christian hope must manifest itself not only in the peace, love, and justice of our relations with others, but also in our relationship with nature. Christian faith condemns not only domestic abuse but also ecological abuse. If oppressing the weak is to oppose the divine designs, the same must be said about the unjust exploitation of nature.

\*      \*      \*

To sum up: Christian hope—what we also call "eschatology"—is a fundamental element in the Christian message. This is so because eschatology isn't a matter of predicting every detail of the future, as if we had a crystal ball such as those employed by charlatans claiming they can tell us exactly what will happen. Rather than predicting the future, Christian hope calls us to live as those who already know what the future holds.

We know what the future holds because the one whom we expect is the one whom we already know: Jesus Christ the Lord. When we refer to the peace of God's reign, this isn't just any peace, but the one that we're already beginning to enjoy thanks to the one who said, "Peace I leave with you; my peace I give to you" (John 14:27). When we speak of justice, we do so in obedience and service to the one who invites us to suffer hunger and thirst for justice. When we speak of love, we do so celebrating the one who out of love came to dwell among us, took the form of a servant, and became like one of us. All this we do, and not out of fear, but because we know that this is the one we expect, and before whom every knee shall bend, "in heaven and on earth and under the earth," and the entire world shall confess that Jesus Christ is Lord (Phil. 2:10–11).

This is why I began this chapter by insisting that eschatology is not a matter of fear, but of hope. This Christian hope tells us that, no matter how much evil we see in the world and no matter how many difficulties stand in our way, our future is in the hands of God. Since we know that this

145

God of our future loves us even more than we love ourselves, we can live lives of hope even in the midst of a world calling us to despair. That is the joy of Christian hope!

## For Reflection and Discussion

1. Have you heard eschatological announcements whose purpose is to frighten people? What do you think of such things? Is it possible for someone to be converted out of fear?

2. Think about the decisions you made yesterday. Note that in each of them you considered not only the past, but also a future, a purpose. The future that you expect leads you to act today in a particular way. Isn't it the same when it comes to eschatological hope?

3. Is it true that an eagerness to know exactly when Jesus will come is actually a way not to have to obey him until the end is at hand?

TEN

# Christian Life

In the preceding chapters we have discussed the main Christian doctrines in a particular order: we began with the doctrine of God and creation, and finished by discussing Christian hope. But we have repeatedly seen that the doctrines that we've been studying aren't mere theoretical teachings, but actually have a significant impact on the way in which we live. Thus, as we come to the end of our study, it is wise to explore the relationship between doctrine and life, because it is in that relationship that faith is actually lived out.

Belief is such that what we believe affects what we do, and what we do or refuse to do affects what we believe. In order to be Christians, it's not enough for us to believe certain things. And it's not enough for us to do certain things. It's quite easy for us to deceive ourselves, thinking that if we affirm certain doctrines, that's enough; or that doing or not doing certain things is enough. But, in truth, both walk hand in hand. True belief must lead to doing. And quite often we don't believe because secretly we know that if we believe, we will have to obey.

For this reason, in this last chapter we'll reflect on the various doctrines we've already studied and how they relate to life. Let's begin with the existence of God. When we discuss whether or not God exists, we're speaking not only about doctrine, but also about the manner in which we are to live. It's quite possible that someone who denies the existence of God does so—perhaps even unwittingly—out of fear that if God does exist, he or she will have to live in a particular way. Atheism isn't just the intellectual conviction of some, because in that very conviction there may well be a desire to live without having to render account to anyone. And frequently believers, at the same time that we claim to believe in God, live as if we don't have to render account to anyone—which is actually a practical form of atheism, no matter how much we speak of God. And it's not just a matter of whether we want to do something or not. It's also a matter of whether we prefer to live as if life has no particular meaning, that ultimately nothing counts, or, on the other hand, we prefer to live a life that has meaning.

Similarly, the doctrine of creation also relates directly to life. Creation tells us, first, that the world around us is good because it is the work of God; and second, that because it is the work of God, we must respect it. The world isn't simply something that's there, like a stone we find along a path. It is the intentional work of the God of love. And not only that, but this God, who always defends the defenseless, also defends the world. Today we're becoming increasingly aware that the damage we do to the earth—polluting the air and the water, cutting down forests, drying wetlands, and injecting gases into land to extract oil—is also damaging our lives—in the growing incidence of cancer and respiratory ailments, droughts and floods, and even earth tremors in areas until recently considered stable. If we truly believe that God is the creator of this world around us, we will also believe that it isn't here simply to be mercilessly exploited.

Regarding this God in whom we believe, we have also seen that this is a triune God—a God in whose very being there is community and love. God, while being one in the strictest and absolute sense, is never alone. The communion among the three persons of the Trinity is such that the three are one. Too often we have dealt with the doctrine of the Trinity as if it were a matter of complex speculation, when in truth we should approach it as guidance for our lives. If even God doesn't exist in sovereign solitude, we humans, made in the image of God, are quite unable to exist in solitude. As God says in Genesis, "It is not good for the man to be alone." True human life is life in community. And the model we must imitate in organizing our communal life is the model of the divine Trinity, in which there is such closeness that the three are one. This means that the deeper our sense of community, and the more we share with one another, the better we will reflect the image of God in us. And, since we're created in the image of God, the more we share, the more human we will be.

This leads us to what we have seen regarding what it means to be human. First of all, God created humankind just as he created trees, mountains, and cattle. We are made out of the same dust, the same matter, as the rest of creation, and we are therefore part of it. But at the same time, God has entrusted us with stewardship over this creation. This means that, while we are part of creation, in a certain way we are also above it. It is here that the doctrine of the image of God in humankind becomes crucial for today's issues, because it means that our lordship is intended to be after the image of the God of love, and therefore must be a lordship in love—or, otherwise stated, that all of creation, not only humankind, is this vast community of which we are part and with which we are called to share.

This in turn takes us to the subject of our fourth chapter, Jesus Christ and the new creation. In Jesus Christ, God shares our humanity. God shares not only what might be our glory, but also our human suffering. Therefore, to believe in Christ is not limited to believing that he is truly God and truly human, but implies and demands that we follow his example of being present not only in peaceful and pleasant places, but also where evil and suffering seem to reign.

The culmination of all this is what we saw in discussing the Holy Spirit and the work of sanctification. If the purpose of God is that we may be able to have closer communion with God, that takes place only because of the presence and work of the Holy Spirit among us. Sanctification is a process that isn't meant to lead us away from others or allow us to claim that we're better than others. Rather, it's a process which, while bringing us closer to God, also brings us closer to this humanity and to this world which God so loved . . .

Finally, as we have seen in the last chapter, Christian hope is a promise of such a nature that it must guide the whole of life. It isn't just a matter of awaiting what will take place in the future, but also of living as those who believe in that promise. This means that a true Christian eschatology, rather than leading to fear, is the compass leading us to peace, justice, and love.

Once again, there is a cyclical relationship between belief and obedience: belief helps us obey, and obedience helps us believe.

The truth, however, is that too frequently we don't believe, or we don't obey, or we do neither. It's so easy to deceive ourselves with doubts and excuses! In Luke 10 we're told of a man who was an expert in matters of Bible and theology who came to Jesus, not really expecting to be taught, but actually planning to put him to the test. What that man did, we still do. We approach one another and ask about beliefs, not in order to learn from and teach each other, but rather to test each other. We ask a sister what she believes not in order to listen to her, but rather to classify her and see to what particular party she belongs. And then we dare criticize that man who approached Jesus in order to test him!

Jesus answers by telling the man what he already knew: "You shall love the Lord your God with all your heart, and with all your soul, and with all your strength, and with all your mind; and your neighbor as yourself" (Luke 10:27). As the man shows, it is always possible to postpone obedience by asking more and more questions. He thus tries to justify himself by asking a question: "And who is my neighbor?" There follows the well-known parable of the good Samaritan, and at the end what Jesus asks the interpreter of the law is not—as we would expect—who helped the neighbor who was lying by the road, but rather who was his neighbor.

The question itself is interesting because a good Jew didn't consider a Samaritan to be a neighbor. And yet, the man is forced to answer that the neighbor of the wounded Jew was the Samaritan who showed mercy to him. There follows the commandment of Jesus: "Go and do likewise."

Let us go and do likewise!

### For Reflection and Discussion

1. Make a list of what you've learned since starting this book and of your reflections and discussions with others. Will any of this somehow enrich your faith and your life?

2. What relationship is there between what you believe and the way you live? Is it true that we live on the basis of what we believe? Or is it rather that we adjust our beliefs to the way in which we wish to live?

3. Now that we've finished this study, how will you share it with others? Do you feel ready to direct a group in the same study? What benefits would you see in such an endeavor, both for yourself and for them?

4. Has this book helped you understand and appreciate Christians of other denominations or traditions? How?

5. As you close this book, pray for its author, for those who have studied it with you, and for all others who may study it in the future. Thank you!

# Index

INDEX